Reading Conversations

Reading Conversations

Retrospective Miscue Analysis with Struggling Readers, Grades 4–12

Rita A. Moore and Carol Gilles

with

*Jennifer Wilson, Karen Brantingham,
Chris Aspegren, and Vicki Seeger*

Foreword by Dorothy J. Watson

HEINEMANN
Portsmouth, NH

Heinemann
361 Hanover Street
Portsmouth, NH 03801–3912
www.heinemann.com

Offices and agents throughout the world

Library of Congress Cataloging-in-Publication Data
Moore, Rita A.
   Reading conversations : retrospective miscue analysis with struggling readers, grades 4–12 / Rita A. Moore and Carol Gilles, with Jennifer Wilson ... [et al.] ; foreword by Dorothy J. Watson.
     p. cm.
   Includes bibliographical references and index.
   ISBN 0-325-00720-9 (alk. paper)
   1. Miscue analysis—Case studies. 2. Reading—Remedial teaching—Case studies. I. Gilles, Carol. II. Title.
LB1050.33.M66 2005
372.48—dc22   2004020854

Editor: James Strickland
Production: Vicki Kasabian
Cover design: Night & Day Design
Typesetter: Kim Arney Mulcahy
Manufacturing: Steve Bernier

Printed in the United States of America on acid-free paper
15 14 13 12 11   VP   7 8 9 10

This book is dedicated to the life and work of Dorothy Watson,
a leader in miscue analysis and possibly the first teacher to use RMA.
Dorothy, a longtime friend and mentor of ours, taught us that
no reading miscue is ever without meaning.

Contents

Foreword

Picture a group of students. Any age, social class, or ethnicity. Privileged or poor. School savvy or street smart. Hostile or helpful. Mentally and physically healthy or ailing. Add any school or societal label used to categorize your group members, who, by the way, have as many or more differences between them than they have with members of other groups.

Now, create a text to accompany your picture. You are a resourceful and creative teacher of reading who knows that to be *honestly* successful in teaching (no "Texas miracle"), you must know as much as possible about your students' strengths and needs. In order to get such information you have to make choices about *what* to learn and *how* to get the information. Two possibilities are offered to you.

Possibility 1: Administer a standardized, high-stakes reading test. *Rationale for choosing Possibility 1:* Your time is limited, a staggering number of students are in your care, standardized tests are relatively fast, and, you rationalize, the pain inflicted on students and yourself will go away over time. (To be realistic, *Possibility 1* may be a mandate, not a choice at all, but let's pretend.) *What you learn:* Some might answer that at best you learn nothing about your students' reading abilities and needs, and at worst you are given false, potentially harmful information. Actually you may learn something. You may learn just how well your inevitable test-prep curriculum pays off on a standardized test.

Possibility 2: After saying no to teaching *for* or *to the test* (even no to mandated tests—a scary and courageous act), you decide to teach *for the students. Rationale for choosing Possibility 2:* Teaching for the students involves an assessment that fits perfectly with your holistic beliefs about learning and learners. Your curriculum and classroom are already organized in such a way that you and your students can thoughtfully consider both their strengths and needs. *What you learn:* More than you might imagine. For starters, you find a reasoned and reasonable place to begin instruction; you discover that with minimal help students are often their own best teachers, and that kids who thought of themselves as losers come to value their own knowledge and ability. You learn that learning and teaching are rewarding and joyful experiences. The authors of *Reading Conversations* help us complete our story by providing information and understanding about an assessment tool, retrospective miscue analysis, that is suited to the beliefs and curriculum of any teacher who chooses *Possibility 2*.

Just as RMA (retrospective miscue analysis) and CRMA (collaborative retrospective miscue analysis) experiences help students revalue themselves as readers, these assessment procedures also help us revalue ourselves as teachers. Often, as teachers we finish some professional books with a feeling of despair and think, "Easy for them to say, but I can't do that." Not so with *Reading Conversations*. Rita and Carol, along with the teachers and students they introduce to us, take us on a heuristic professional journey. Even more important, they bring us back home from that journey. We return more confident in ourselves and greatly enriched with tangible and appropriate assessment and teaching possibilities. These authors help us become retrospective about language, about reading strategies, about learners, and unquestionably about our teaching.

Not only do the authors carefully guide us in understanding how to *do* retrospective miscue analysis, they provide us with the research and theory that supports the doing. We are not asked to borrow an assessment technique; rather we are provided with the information and experiences that enable us to *own* the process of real reading evaluation. When there is ownership, teachers are empowered, students are included rather than excluded from the teaching process, and there is a feeling that what really matters is being evaluated. Additionally, as we read the stories that reflect real language and thought, we witness an excitement and joy in learning and teaching in both students and teachers. Compare this to kids and teachers who hate to come to school on test and test-prep days.

In *Reading Conversations* Rita and Carol provide a means of truly leaving no child and no teacher behind, or leaving them in the dark, or making them sick on test days. Enjoy the journey.

Dorothy J. Watson

Acknowledgments

The authors gratefully acknowledge the research and work of the following teachers, friends, and colleagues: Jennifer Wilson, Karen Brantingham, Chris Aspegren, and Vicki Seeger. Their classroom research in RMA and CRMA is featured throughout this book. Without their classroom stories, this book would not have been written. Many other teachers have contributed their words and thoughts as well. Others, like the preservice teachers in Rita's Literacy and Assessment class and Carol's Language Arts Book Group, have given us valuable feedback from a classroom perspective. Martille Eaton's attention to detail and careful editing are greatly appreciated. We also wish to thank Terre Folger, Patricia Watson, Kathryn Mitchell Pierce, and Patricia Jenkins for their assistance and advice and Dorothy Watson for contributing the foreword.

1

An Invitation to Retrospective Miscue Analysis

I'm trying RMA and it is working like nothing else has for my struggling readers. They are no longer threatened by failure.
                    —Samantha, a High School Special Education Teacher

This chapter will

- introduce and define the retrospective miscue analysis (RMA) process;
- discuss the benefits of RMA for students and teachers;
- provide a brief research rationale for RMA, including the role of talk in learning to read;
- explain collaborative retrospective miscue analysis (CRMA) as an extension of RMA; and
- introduce the teachers and students highlighted throughout the book.

The RMA Process

In the quote above, Samantha echoes the discovery of many teachers who use retrospective miscue analysis: they see marked changes in their students' reading and thinking processes. These teachers realize that reading is more than decoding words; it involves making sense of text using a variety of appropriate strategies—a process that often confounds struggling readers. Using RMA helps students better understand the reading process and become more proficient readers (Goodman and Marek 1996). Those who struggle need to understand that reading is a process of making meaning. They must learn to trust their own intuitive understanding of how language works—what sounds right, what does not, and why.

We believe that social interaction and talk are integral to understanding what it means to read. Conversations about reading lead children to greater literacy as they begin to recognize and use the reading strategies of confident and motivated readers. These conversations, called *retrospective miscue analysis*, or

RMA for short, may be held between a teacher and the reader or in a small group with the teacher guiding the talk. During these conversations readers discover why they miscued, if they needed to correct their miscues, and what reading strategies were effective in helping them monitor for meaning. For students and teachers alike, the analysis process is informative and enjoyable because there is no competition for one correct answer; what the reader has to say is validated by the RMA partner or partners.

The process of RMA is a two-part sequence: an initial reading and retelling session is followed by a conversation about the reading and the retelling. During the initial session, a student reads aloud from a challenging text while the teacher listens to and marks the *miscues*—the unexpected responses to text in the oral reading. This session is known as conducting a *miscue analysis*. (Chapter 3 explains how to conduct a basic miscue analysis.) Some examples of miscues are substitutions, insertions, and omissions. Following the reading, the reader gives an oral summary of the text, called a *retelling*, and the teacher notes patterns in the miscues and retelling to discuss at a later RMA session.

The second part of the process is the RMA session in which the teacher encourages the reader, first, to examine his miscues to determine whether or not they changed the meaning of the text and, second, to decide what strategies might be most effective in helping him monitor for meaning. This is a conversation between and among readers (teacher and students). Participants help one another understand the reasoning behind a miscue or discuss details from a retelling. Following are the fundamental questions asked by both teachers and readers during RMA conversations:

- Did the miscue change the meaning of the text?
- What does the miscue reveal about the reader's knowledge and use of language?
- What was the reader thinking at the time he made the miscue?

Through these conversations, readers quickly learn the terminology associated with RMA as well as the kinds of questions that help them better understand the reading process and themselves as readers.

The Benefits of RMA for Students and Teachers

In our work with readers, we have noted several benefits from RMA for both students and teachers. Most importantly, RMA changes how students view the reading process. When readers are invited to discover their own miscues, analyze them, and talk about why they made them, they realize that reading is not just pronouncing words correctly; it is creating meaning by integrating the author's text with their own background knowledge and experiences.

Readers gain a greater control of expository and narrative texts by problem solving their way through a text as they listen to and interpret their use of reading strategies. They also learn about various strategies from one another. For example, Devon was a seventh-grade reader who always skipped parts of the text. Matt, his RMA partner, told him that he, too, skipped words when he read, but that he kept the words in the back of his mind and later returned to solve them after he had more information. Devon was impressed with his friend's use of that strategy and eventually used it himself.

RMA provides valuable insight into how readers use their knowledge of language to construct meaning while they read. The process of talking about their own oral reading miscues and text retellings with peers, teachers, or both helps children and adolescents gain a greater understanding of themselves as readers. Readers feel empowered and revalued as they gain control of their reading. Samantha, a high school special education teacher, explains:

> Kirk really got into talking about his own miscues—he was in charge and there was no right or wrong answer. He was pretty fascinated by some of his own miscues—finding out what they meant about himself as a reader was a real eye-opener.

Kirk found that many of his miscues made sense, particularly when he examined the personal, social, or knowledge connections he had made to the text. Such insights made him more interested in reading and more aware (metacognitive) of his own reading process.

RMA provides benefits to teachers as well as students. Teachers who use miscue analysis realize what a powerful tool it is for both assessment and instruction. Miscue analysis provides valuable information about student reading behaviors that can be used to plan instruction in other contexts such as guided reading or minilessons about reading strategies. RMA takes reading instruction one step further by engaging the reader in conversations about his own miscues with teachers, classmates, or both. RMA helps the teacher understand what the reader was thinking at the time of the miscue. Knowing the reasoning behind the miscue opens a new window on the reading process. Teachers may *think* they know their students, but until they listen to readers explore and explain their miscues, important insights into the readers' knowledge and use of language go untapped.

Teachers who learn to implement RMA in their reading instruction gain greater insights into the reading process. And they become much better at both reflection and diagnosis of reading strengths and weaknesses (Worsnop 1996). For example, Julie, a second-grade teacher, talks about Stan, with whom she has been using RMA for more than a year both in the classroom and during her extended work with him in after-school tutoring:

> It is interesting doing RMA with Stan; he does it on the spot. As he reads, he will recognize the miscue as an error, usually by saying aloud, "That's not _____," or "That does not make sense." I've noticed when he retells the story he's starting to use the author's words in his retellings; he has an ear for details and his comprehension is high.

Julie knows a lot more about each one of her readers than she did before using RMA. She is observing reading responses and behaviors that she might have otherwise overlooked.

Teachers who look at miscues as evidence of how the reader is constructing meaning will never listen to a child read in the same way again. More importantly, teachers who listen to children use talk to explore the meaning behind their miscues may never teach in the same way again.

RMA Is Supported by the Research

In the midst of current state and federal demands to have scientifically based reading curricula, there is a wealth of research supporting RMA (see Appendix H). Since no miscue is without meaning, RMA is a process of "revaluing" the reader (Goodman 1996b, 15). Teachers using RMA recognize existing as well as potential reading strengths, thus helping learners identify reading strategies that will prove more effective than those they may currently use. The premise behind RMA underscores Vygotsky's theory of the zone of proximal development (ZPD), the distance between what the child is able to do independently and the child's level of potential development—what the child is able to do under the guidance of an adult or a more capable peer (Vygotksy 1978, 68). Through RMA, readers benefit from knowledgeable others and from social interactions leading to new understandings; this situation places the learner in an environment that validates the worth and potential of the reader. Learners are empowered to discuss the reading process by analyzing their own miscues.

Retrospective miscue analysis is based on knowledge about reading and learning as well as on a strong knowledge about social interaction and talk. We know that talk is a powerful motivator for students. When Goodlad (1984) asked middle school students why they came to school, the most common answer was to talk to friends. Through their talk in small groups, students see immediate examples of what reading strategies others use. They work together to problem solve their way through difficult miscues. As readers help one another and build on each other's ideas, they are using the hesitant, rough-draft, "exploratory talk," a concept introduced in the work of Barnes (1992) and further discussed in Chapter 6. Readers share with others what they were thinking as they read, why they might have miscued, and if the miscues needed correction. This kind of talk prompts readers to become more metacognitive throughout the reading process. As they bring their own reading process and that of others to a conscious level, readers are more open to trying new and more effective reading strategies.

Collaborative Retrospective Miscue Analysis

Collaborative retrospective miscue analysis is an extension of RMA piloted by Sarah Costello in 1992. While both RMA and CRMA are reader centered, CRMA conversations are directed by readers, not the teacher. The goal of CRMA is for students to gain greater independence and confidence as readers who are able to confidently discuss miscues and textual interpretation. Conversation, or talk, among readers is serious and focused on exploring, defining, and expanding their knowledge of themselves as readers and learners.

Briefly, CRMA groups are composed of two to six students, usually in the intermediate grades or high school, with mixed or similar reading proficiencies. The teacher defines the composition of the group. These students facilitate discussion about their miscues and retellings. The students must have previous experience in RMA, understand the miscue coding, and know the RMA procedures to be successful. The teacher monitors the CRMA conversation and may step in to point out inconsistencies or direct attention to proficient use of reading strategies; however, she need not be present at all times. Going from RMA, which is teacher guided, to CRMA, which is student directed, generally involves a gradual release of responsibility, especially with struggling or nonconfident readers. (CRMA and its relationship to RMA are discussed in greater detail in Chapter 6.)

Voices from the Field: Featured Teachers and Readers Who Benefited from RMA

Throughout this book, RMA conversations between and among teachers and struggling readers highlight research inquiries conducted in elementary, intermediate, and secondary classrooms. We focus on the voices of the teachers and students to help readers think about how they might find ways of including RMA and

CRMA in their own classrooms. The following teachers shared their RMA or CRMA experiences with us:

Karen Brantingham is a reading specialist who integrated RMA conversations into the reading curriculum for the fourth-grade students in her Title I reading classroom. Justin, Nathan, and Steve were struggling, nonconfident boys who all read below grade level. Justin was failing reading in his classroom; Nathan struggled with oral reading; and Steve's motivation and comprehension were minimal. As will be discussed in Chapter 5, their lack of progress in response to a variety of reading programs and strategies puzzled their classroom teachers.

Jennifer Wilson, a former middle school teacher, is a doctoral student at the University of Missouri. Jennifer used RMA with Matt and Devon, two seventh-grade boys labeled learning disabled. Both boys lacked confidence and strategies in reading. They initially believed that they were reading failures, but Jennifer built their trust in the reading process through RMA and later led them into CRMA. In Chapter 3 we use Matt's and Devon's miscues to explain the miscue analysis procedure, while in Chapter 7 we discuss their work with Jennifer.

Chris Aspegren is a high school language arts teacher in an alternative school setting. For several years Chris experimented with RMA conversations between the teacher and individual students as well as among students. Her first RMA project was with Dan, a high school senior (Moore and Aspegren 2001). We use some of Dan's comments to explain RMA in Chapter 4. As a result of her work with Dan, Chris now uses information from individual miscue analyses and retellings for RMA. Her students also independently hold conversations about texts (CRMA). With the help of her students, Chris fashioned a reading curriculum built upon RMA and CRMA strategies. The students in Chapter 8, Brad, Luke, and Roy, are older teens whose histories include academic and social failure. When they entered Chris' class they all read fairly fluently in a grade-level text but had trouble making connections to text at a more than surface level. Through understanding themselves as readers, they became capable of interpreting text, and all three found success both academically and socially in that they learned to value and respect the comments and interpretations of the CRMA group members.

Vicki Seeger, a fifth-grade classroom teacher, is conducting a classroom RMA research study for the first time with a group of struggling readers: Suzanne, Thomas, Katie, and Rene. Vicki is trying to move Suzanne and Thomas beyond phonetic decoding and word chunking to strategies such as using context clues, skipping ahead, and returning. Katie repeats herself consistently while reading but has good comprehension, while Rene is a fluent reader with low comprehension. Examples from Vicki's work are woven throughout the book.

These teachers and students provide evidence that listening to and talking with readers from grades 4 through 12 about their reading miscues and the rationale behind them can positively affect reading performance and attitude.

Summing It Up and Moving On

RMA and CRMA conversations provide elementary and secondary teachers with two practical and highly effective approaches to improving students' reading. Not one-size-fits-all models of instruction, these approaches provide specific strategies for assessment and instruction unlike those found in traditional reading texts. Using RMA and CRMA procedures, students and teachers explore reading as a meaning-making process by questioning, examining, and making decisions about reading miscues and students' retelling of text. These highly adaptable procedures may be employed in reading workshop, guided reading, and literature discussion groups and may be used for individual assessment.

RMA does not require expensive commercial materials. Students talk about the reading process by discussing their own reading miscues and examining their retellings of text. Through these conversations, students gain greater understanding of how their own reading processes and text work together to help them make gains in fluency, comprehension, and vocabulary skills.

Chapter 2 examines the foundation of RMA—the systems of language and the reading process. Directions for conducting an initial miscue analysis, marking the miscues, scoring the retelling guides, and creating an RMA organizer to prepare for the conversations are explained in detail in Chapter 3. Chapter 4 outlines the use of the RMA process as an assessment and instructional tool. Chapter 5 discusses the value and purpose of conducting RMA conversations with struggling intermediate readers with varying abilities and perceptions of themselves as readers. Chapter 6 explains collaborative RMA, while Chapter 7 explores how one teacher helped her middle school students transition from RMA into CRMA and revalue themselves as readers. Chapter 8 explores CRMA as an instructional strategy with high school students within an alternative setting. Many of the ideas found in the chapters about older readers can easily be transferred to younger students and vice versa, so we encourage readers to explore information from each chapter that may be applicable to a variety of classroom settings. Chapter 9 includes frequently asked questions about RMA and Chapter 10 offers some concluding thoughts on RMA and CRMA as assessment and instructional processes. Reproducible forms and other helpful guides are included in the appendices.

2

Processes That Form
the Foundation for RMA

*I've wanted to try RMA for some time, but the miscue analysis
scares me a little.*

—Vicki, a Fifth-Grade Teacher

This chapter will

- introduce miscues and the concepts supporting miscue analysis;
- discuss the reading process and the systems of language (also known as *cueing systems*) foundational to miscue analysis and RMA; and
- introduce the Burke Reading Interview as one way to gather information from readers about their perceptions of the reading process.

Vicki's concern about using miscue analysis is understandable. The term *miscue analysis* sounds complicated and difficult to some teachers. However, we have found that understanding the concepts behind miscue analysis makes the process easier and clearer. Miscue analysis offers teachers a natural way to gather important information about children's strengths in reading and to make decisions about what strategies readers need to use in order to help them be more *effective* and *efficient*. Effective readers read for meaning. Efficient readers make sense using "the least amount of time and effort"; they "leap toward meaning using information from background, perceptions, and predictions" (Davenport 2002,13).

What Is a Miscue and How Does Miscue Analysis Work?

A miscue is a reader's variation from print—that is, anything the reader says that does not match the text. The goal of miscue analysis is to "describe, explain and evaluate a reader's control or ownership of the [reading] process" (Goodman, Watson, and Burke 1987, 3). In miscue analysis, teachers and/or researchers listen to a student read an unfamiliar passage of narrative or expository text, mark the unexpected responses (miscues), and then code and analyze them to find patterns in the student's reading behavior.

Miscue analysis is based on two important concepts: (1) everyone miscues (deviates from the written text) and (2) miscues do not equal errors (Watson 1996a). Miscues include a continuum of unexpected responses, from those that do not change the meaning of the text to those that change the meaning considerably. All people—children, adolescents, and adults—make miscues. One of our colleagues remembers that she couldn't understand as a child why they sang "scared" music in church. It was, of course, *sacred* music. Another colleague complained that her husband never stopped when they were on long car trips. On one such trip, after four hours in the car, exhausted and hungry, she spotted a road sign she read as "Pizza ahead." She motioned to her husband to stop. "That's not 'pizza,'" he countered, "that's *Peoria* ahead." Her hunger had colored her perceptions and caused a miscue.

Try to spot miscues at a meeting where someone reads the minutes aloud while you follow along in the printed text. Although the adult reader may make a number of changes from the text, most of the variations will not change the meaning. Instead, the reader will probably translate the text into language that is a bit more comfortable or natural. Proficient readers may substitute "a" for *the* or move text around slightly. Goodman and Marek (1996) call miscues that do not change the meaning *high-quality* miscues, while those that do change the meaning are *low quality*. We have found when working with students that they more easily understand the terms *high level* and *low level* as descriptions for miscues. For example, consider how Matt (a seventh grader whose story is told in Chapter 7) read the following:

$$\overset{\text{to}}{}$$

1005   when you go into a cave in June or July, be sure to look for baby

Matt substituted "to" for *into*. Because Matt's miscue does not change the meaning considerably, we call it a high-level miscue. Though a detailed discussion of miscue analysis procedures appears in Chapter 3, a quick overview will provide some context here. In miscue analysis, the teacher asks the student to read an unfamiliar text that has a beginning, a middle, and an end and is somewhat challenging. The teacher audiotapes the session and marks all of the reader's miscues on a typescript while the student reads. At the end of the reading, the teacher asks the student to retell the story to gain an overall sense of the student's understanding. Teachers often use a retelling protocol that assigns points for plot development, characters, setting, and theme to assess the student's comprehension. After the session, the teacher checks the markings for accuracy while listening to the tape and codes each of the miscues to determine the relationship of the miscues to the systems of language. Taking a close look at the miscues and the retelling helps the teacher understand the strategies the reader used or ignored. Did Nathan decode slowly and miss the meaning of the story? Did Matt look at the beginning letter of unknown words and guess—that is, was he overdependent on graphic information? Did Dan monitor his reading? Did Suzanne supply words that fit the grammar of the sentence but were not meaningful, thereby using the syntax of the sentence but not the semantics? Analyzing the miscues and tallying the results help the teacher better understand how students read and what might be done to assist them in becoming efficient and effective readers.

Connecting Miscue Analysis to the Reading Process and Systems of Language

Miscue analysis is a powerful procedure based on more than forty years of research on the reading process, linguistics, reader response, and psychology. For a summary of the research, see Appendix H.

Reading Strategies Within the Reading Process

First introduced in 1968, miscue analysis is predicated on the idea that reading is more than orally decoding, or reproducing each word in the text as it is written. Kenneth Goodman has consistently refined his model of the reading process (1984, 1994, 1996). Building on his model, we have represented the strategies that readers use as a series of spirals within the context of the reading event. (See Figure 2–1.)

Goodman suggests that readers *sample* from text and *predict* the next feature or plot event in the text. Because language is redundant and predictable, efficient readers use what they need to make meaning, instead of consciously processing every grapheme (a significant unit of written language). They use their background information, predictions, and key visual information to make sense of the text.

To test sampling at work, see how many vanity car license plates you can decipher correctly. Readers can make meaning from sequences without vowels, like "I lv skr" (I love soccer), because they rely more on consonants than vowels for meaning (Weaver, Gillmeister-Krause, and Vento-Zogby 1996, 33). Another simple test demonstrates that readers predict. The next time you are reading a novel, say the next few words on the following page *before* turning the page. Were you right? Did you predict what was to come? Most people are able to predict the next few words of a text, based on the meaning of the piece and the redundancy of language. Of course, the more familiar the reader is with the topic, the easier this is to do.

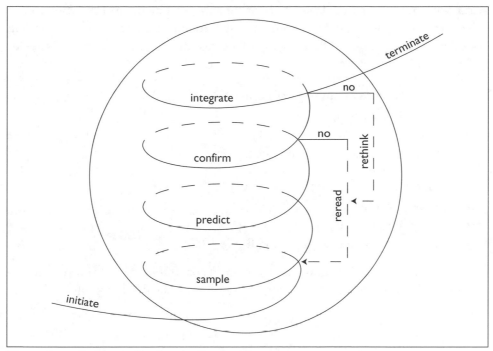

Figure 2–1. Strategies Used in the Reading Process

As readers continue in the text, they *confirm* the predictions they have made with the actual text. Then they *integrate* the meaning they have formed from their background experiences with the author's meaning, thereby creating a meaning for the text (Goodman 1984, 1994; Rosenblatt [1938] 1976). If readers fail to make meaning, they have the option to resample, rethink, repredict, and then integrate or to stop their reading. Readers who monitor their understanding know when they need to slow down, reread, or repredict.

Understanding the reading process is important to miscue analysis and RMA because proficient and nonproficient readers all depend on the same process. The difference in their success is due to how well they control their reading process to construct meaning (Goodman and Marek 1996). The reading process is tied closely to the systems of language, or cueing systems.

Systems of Language

Knowing the systems of language helps teachers understand the features readers use well and those they don't use proficiently or ignore as they read. Understanding how a reader uses the systems of language makes it easier for a teacher to build a program that fits that reader's needs. Although Ken Goodman (1996) now considers pragmatics as a part of the semantic system, for discussion purposes we will consider them separately. The systems of language include three linguistic systems and three pragmatic systems:

Linguistic Systems (language systems)
- semantic (meaning)
- syntactic (structure or grammar)
- graphophonic (sound-symbol relationships)

Pragmatic Systems ("language in use")
- context of situation
- background knowledge
- culture (Goodman, Watson, and Burke 1987)

These systems work together as a student reads. In Figure 2–2 the systems are represented as concentric circles. The dotted lines indicate that each of the sys-

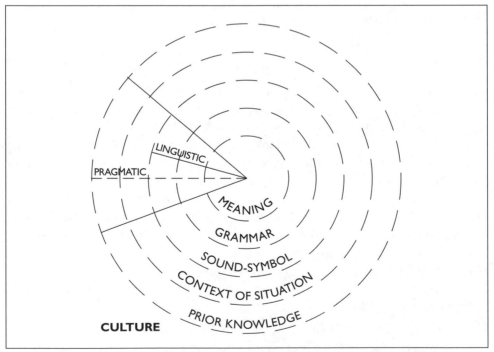

Figure 2–2. Pragmatic and Linguistic Systems of Language (Watson, Burke, and Y. Goodman in Gilles et al. 1988)

tems depends on the others for support. Culture is outside the circles, indicating that it permeates all of the other systems.

Linguistic systems   Examining how a reader uses the linguistic systems gives teachers valuable information about how students use knowledge of language in their reading. These cueing systems include information about how the reader uses meaning, the structure of the sentence (grammar), and visual information. Teachers can use miscue analysis or running records to assess these systems (Clay 2000).

Making meaning is the purpose of reading and is crucial to the process; thus, the *semantic* system is at the heart of the systems of language. For example, a beginning teacher early in the school year listened to each one of her fifth-grade students read to determine individual reading abilities. One child, Anna, read the passage perfectly, using fairly good intonation and making no miscues. However, when the teacher asked her to retell the passage, Anna replied, "No habla inglés!" Anna could decode—sound out the words in the passage—but since her first language was Spanish and she spent only a few months each year in the United States, she had almost no understanding of what she read. Anna was not an effective reader. Even though she read without miscues, she was not constructing meaning while reading.

More typically, students who are not gaining meaning pronounce nonwords that may look like the text. When they read something that does not fit the meaning of the story and do not pause, a teacher can later ask, "Did that make sense?" This is an important question that relies on the semantic system. This question is used in retrospective miscue analysis and in other one-on-one work with students.

All meaning is inscribed on the structure of the language—the *syntax*, or grammar. Children come to school with an innate grammatical knowledge of English. They know that in the sentence "John ran down the _____," the word in the blank has to be a word like *street* or *stairs* (nouns). It can't be *running* (verb) or some other part of speech. Readers use this innate knowledge as they read. Syntax includes the surface structures, "the relationships signaled by word endings, function words, and word order," and also the deep structure, "the underlying relations among words of a sentence" (Weaver 1980, 22). When readers take the surface structure and translate it into a more comfortable deep structure, they are using the syntactic system. For example, Watson (1996b, 17) reports this miscue:

Stop. Wait a moment, Timber.   *(minute written above moment)*

The student translated *moment* into a more comfortable structure, "minute," without changing the meaning. If readers make miscues that are nonwords but look like the text word, and do not stop to correct, teachers can ask them, "Does that sound like language?" This question helps readers focus on the syntactic system.

Of course reading cannot happen without the squiggles on the page, the *grapho-phonemes*. The letters, the white spaces between them, the font, the size of print, and so on, all give readers information about what the message might be. However, the more background readers have on the topic and the better predictions they make, the less they actually depend on the graphophonemes. Consider the reading that people do for fun. When readers stretch out with a good mystery or a rousing adventure story, they do not carefully examine every letter of every word. Instead, they skim as much as needed to create meaning until they get to the juicy parts, where they slow down and read more carefully. If information is new, readers are likely to read more slowly and spend more time with the graphophonics or sound-symbol associations. Many people depend more on the actual text when reading a tax form than when reading a novel of choice.

Pragmatic systems   While the features of the linguistic systems are vitally important, the aspects of the pragmatic systems also can inform teachers. *Pragmatic* means language in use; the pragmatic systems include a reader's background experience, the context of situation, and the culture.

Context of situation refers to expectations of readers and intentions of authors (Watson 1988). People form expectations based on past experiences. For example, customers who frequent fine restaurants expect cloth napkins, fine china, and a lot of silverware on the table. In their experiences with restaurants, these features signal, if not a delicious meal, certainly an expensive one! Likewise, children who have had fairy tales read to them expect that a new tale will begin "Once upon a time" and end "happily ever after." In their experiences with the fairy tale genre, "once upon a time" has occurred frequently. Discussing the structures students might expect in certain texts or genres can help them navigate a text more easily. If students know that science texts often are structured around specific vocabulary and explanations, they can make better decisions about reading the texts more effectively.

Background of experience is crucial to making meaning. Readers bring their own background knowledge to the reading episode and integrate it with the words on the page to create meaning; thus, the more background about the topic a reader has, the easier it will be to make logical predictions, monitor, and create appropriate meanings. Consider how you read something familiar. Is it easy? Enjoyable? Now, think about something unfamiliar, perhaps economics or philosophy. Is it more difficult and less enjoyable? When readers know little about the topic, the vocabulary becomes more problematic and predictions are less sure. Thus helping students build background through prereading discussions about the illustrations, characters, language patterns, and story structure is essential to their reading with meaning (Fountas and Pinnell 1996).

A reader's *culture* surrounds all of the systems of language. An analogous situation to the role culture plays in reading is the netting that beekeepers wear when they work with bees. The netting acts as a filter. Bees cannot come in, but the beekeeper's words and facial movements are also filtered to others through the netting. Similarly, everything readers hear or say is filtered through their own culture. When reading passages do not reflect a reader's culture, they are more difficult to read. Consider this short piece:

Twenty20 Ashes Clash Gets Boards' Approval

England and Australia's boards have provisionally agreed to play a Twenty20-style international during next summer's Ashes series. It is believed that the one-off match had been prompted by the huge popularity of the format in its first season last year, when more than 250,000 spectators thronged the county grounds. . . .

But not everyone was enthusiastic. Dean Jones, the former Australian batsman, told the Age: "It's cheapening one-day cricket a little bit for me. The bash-artists are the only ones who get a game. But it's an interesting concept." (Cricinfo 2004, 1)

Was the piece easy to read or difficult? Take a moment to think about what made it difficult. Most people find difficulty with vocabulary that is not used as we expect (*20/20* is a news program), unknown vocabulary (*one-off match*), and a lack of familiarity with the topic (cricket). Yet, this passage was taken from a sports news website on June 10, 2004, in Australia. It is written for grade school children and adults. And it is in English! Imagine how speakers of other languages who live in the United States struggle with the cultural overtones of literature written by Americans! Everything people read is culture laden.

Readers use *all* of the linguistic and pragmatic features as they read. Dorothy Watson explains, "Within the complexly organized systems of language there are subsystems that work in concert to help humans organize their experiences and mediate meaning" (1988, 5). All of these systems work together, not in isolation, to help readers construct meaning.

The reading strategies described earlier continually interact with the subsystems. When students read, they sample from print and make predictions. Their predictions are based on their background, their culture, the situational context, and specific linguistic systems. They use the letters, the white spaces, and the shape of the words, as well as the structure of the sentence and the meaning of the word and/or the sentence, to help them predict the next structure. When they confirm, they again check the syntactic and semantic acceptability of the sentence. They then integrate the author's meaning with their own background of meaning and comprehend the text (D. Goodman 1996).

The ultimate purpose of the retrospective miscue analysis is to help readers learn to control these reading strategies of sampling, predicting, confirming, and integrating meaning. RMA asks specific questions that bring the reader's knowledge of the semantic, syntactic, and graphophonemic systems to conscious awareness. In essence, RMA encourages readers to be more metacognitive, that is, able to talk about their thinking. Asking readers questions such as "Did that make sense?" focuses their attention on the semantic/meaning system. Asking, "Did that sound like language?" focuses their attention on the syntactic/grammar system. Once readers examine the reading process and talk about it, they are better able to gain control of it, make more meaningful, high-level miscues, and diminish the number of low-level miscues that interfere with the reading process.

The Burke Reading Interview

Before giving the miscue analysis, many teachers use the Burke Reading Interview (Burke 1987) to identify students' perceived reading behaviors and attitudes. The Burke Reading Interview has a number of questions that reveal a reader's model of reading, his self-efficacy, the strategies he uses, the books he has read, and the prior instruction he has received. Figure 2–3 is Matt's Burke Interview. He is one of the seventh-grade boys who worked with Jennifer Wilson. Chapter 7 discusses their work together. Jennifer also asked questions to follow up on Matt's answers, thus maintaining a conversational tone in the informal interview setting. Matt's answers are in italics and Jennifer's prompts are in parentheses. A form of the Burke Reading Interview can be found in Appendix A.

The first question contains an example of prior instruction. Instead of saying that he sounds a word out or skips it, Matt mentions the five-finger rule that he has been taught. Students hold up one finger for each word in the story they do not know. If they raise five fingers, the book is too difficult for them. Even when Jennifer suggests that if Matt figures out the word as he reads he can put the finger down, he does not agree. Oftentimes struggling readers hang on to parts of ideas, strategies, and procedures a favorite teacher has taught them, even if they may be incorrect or counterproductive. Matt depends on sounding out the word (question 6) or skipping it (question 1). Even as a seventh grader he doesn't read nonfiction. And the only book he can remember is *Holes* (Sachar 1998), which was read aloud earlier by the teacher.

Using the Burke Interview as a starting place helps teachers to better know readers. They can then compare the readers' perceptions of their behavior with what they actually do while reading. Some readers say what they think the teacher wants to hear, while others are quite honest. Many young readers have not thought about what they do as readers; they are less metacognitive. For these readers, the Burke Interview answers are more a reflection of what they have been taught.

Burke Reading Interview

Name: *Matt*   Age: *14*   Date: *10-05-01*

Grade level: *7th grade*   Sex: *male*   Interviewer: *Jennifer Wilson*

1. When you are reading and you come to something you don't know, what do you do? *I use the five-finger rule.* (What's that?) *Well when I come to a word I don't know, I put one of my fingers up and then I skip it and then I read the rest of the sentence and then I go back.* (If you get the word, do you put the finger down or leave it up?) *Leave it up.* (Do you do anything else?) *No.* (Do you do anything different when you read nonfiction?) *I don't read true stuff.*

2. Who is a good reader that you know? *Duran* [a friend in special education].

3. What makes Duran a good reader? *He likes to read.*

4. Do you think that he ever comes to something that he doesn't know when he is reading? *Sometimes.*

5. When he does come to something unknown, what do you think he does about it? *I don't know.*

6. If you knew that someone was having difficulty reading, how would you help that person? *Tell them to find a word that's in the word that they don't know and then try to sound it out and stuff.*

7. What would your teacher do to help that person? *Same thing.*

8. How did you learn to read? *Don't know.*

9. What would you like to do better as reader? *Try to get some more things read.*

10. Do you think that you are a good reader? *Sorta.* Why? *Because of all the times I practice.*

11. If someone asked you to get something fun to read, what would you pick? <u>Holes</u>.

12. Is there anything else you want to tell me about your reading? *Nope.*

Figure 2–3. Matt's Burke Reading Interview

Summing It Up and Moving On

The keys to the questions and procedures used in RMA are found in the systems of language and the reading process. RMA helps students gain control of the reading process by bringing questions from the systems of language to a conscious level. As readers reflect on their miscues and those systems, they become able to monitor their own reading and can make better processing decisions. The next chapter will more fully explain the process of giving a miscue analysis, marking the typescript, and placing miscues on the RMA organizer to prepare for the conversation.

3

Marking and Coding Miscues
for RMA Conversations

I didn't know I was that kind of reader. You know, a good reader.
—Matt, a Seventh Grader

This chapter will

- explain how to conduct a miscue analysis and retelling to prepare for retrospective miscue analysis conversations and
- offer procedures on marking and coding miscues to place on the RMA organizer.

Note: If you have had extensive experiences with miscue analysis, you may wish to read this chapter quickly. If you have some expertise with running records, but not with miscue analysis, you will find the two procedures somewhat similar, but you will need to review this chapter. If you have little knowledge of running records or miscue analysis, you will need to read this chapter carefully before proceeding. Reading Miscue Inventory: From Evaluation to Instruction for All Readers (Goodman, Watson, and Burke 2005) is an excellent resource should you wish to read more detailed information.

Miscue Analysis Procedure

Miscue analysis is a powerful tool that gives teachers and students a "window on the reading process" (Goodman 1973). Through miscue analysis, Matt discovered that he might be "you know, a good reader." In order to describe a miscue analysis procedure, we will discuss Jennifer Wilson's work with Matt, whose Burke Reading Interview was described in Chapter 2, and Devon, another of her students. Figure 3–1 contains a quick summary of the steps involved in the procedure.

Miscue Analysis

1. Select texts to use for miscue analysis and get equipment ready.
2. Create typescript on which to mark miscues. Either type one or photocopy and enlarge the original.
3. Make your reader comfortable and give the instructions. Don't forget to turn on the tape recorder.
4. Mark the typescript as the reader reads.
5. Conduct the retelling. Include an aided retelling to get as much information as possible.
6. Prepare the RMA organizer.
7. Plan a program of study for your reader.

Figure 3–1. Quick Guide to Miscue Analysis Procedure

1. Selecting a text   The text used for miscue analysis should be at least 250 to 500 words (depending on the age and ability of the reader), cohesive, interesting, and challenging. The purpose of miscue analysis is to observe and describe how the reader processes text. If the passage is too familiar or easy, there will be little to analyze. Jennifer consulted with Matt's reading teacher to determine Matt's ability. She then selected one text that was somewhat challenging for him, one slightly easier text, and one more difficult text. Jennifer brought all three texts to the session because she knew she might need to change texts, moving up or down in difficulty depending on Matt's reading. Jennifer also brought a tape recorder to tape the session; this allowed her to listen to the reading again to make sure her markings were correct.

2. Creating a typescript   Before conducting the reading session, Jennifer created a typescript from the selected text. She had two alternatives for doing this. If time were short, she could have photocopied the text and enlarged it to at least 125 percent, so that there would be space between the lines to record the miscues. (Copyright law permits one copy for educational purposes.) For Matt's session, she typed out the text. She numbered each line beginning with 0101 (meaning page 1, line 1). Text page 3 began 0301 on the typescript. Jennifer triple-spaced the typescript in order to have ample space to record miscues. Figure 3–5 (page 31) shows a portion of a marked typescript.

3. Instructing the student   Jennifer checked that a blank tape was properly loaded and that the tape recorder was in working order. She provided Matt with the original text, while she used the typescript for marking and coding. Jennifer first asked

Matt to look through the story in order to familiarize himself with the length and difficulty of the text. She then read the title of the story to him and asked Matt to read the story aloud. She said, "Pretend that I'm not here and do what you would do normally. After you have read the entire story aloud, I'll ask you to retell it to me, so you need to read to remember." Then she had to adhere to her instructions! If Matt paused in the reading, Jennifer counted the seconds, placed a P (for pause) on the transcript, and recorded how long he stopped. She did not supply the word. When Matt stopped and looked to her for support, she reminded him to do what he would do if she were not there. She did not offer help. Teachers who are familiar with running records may find this part of the procedure different from that of running records. In miscue analysis the teacher allows readers sufficient time to consider their strategies. After a pause of approximately one minute, the teacher reminds the reader to do whatever he would do if he were reading alone.

After Matt had read about a page, Jennifer realized that the first piece she selected was too difficult. She instructed him to finish reading the page and then asked him to retell the story so far. Sometimes teachers find that even with a large number of miscues, readers have considerable understanding of the text. Or, conversely, a reader with few or no miscues may not understand the piece at all. Jennifer decided Matt's story was too difficult because he made numerous miscues and could tell her very little about the portion he had read. Jennifer told Matt that she had made an error in the reading selection for him and would like him to try another story that might work better. The next, easier piece gave her a good sampling of his reading and retelling abilities.

4. Marking the typescript   As Matt read, Jennifer marked the typescript, noting as many of his miscues as she could. (See Figure 3–2 for a miscue marking guide.) Teachers familiar with running records or informal reading inventories find the miscue markings somewhat similar to the markings used in those procedures. However, unlike for running records, teachers do not make a check for every correct word in miscue marking. Instead, they mark only responses that deviate from the text. For example, if Matt attempted a word three times, Jennifer recorded each attempt above the word on the typescript. For ease in describing how to mark miscues, we have borrowed Goodman, Watson, and Burke's (1987) terminology. We call the text item the *expected response* (ER) and what the reader says the *observed response* (OR). We include basic miscue markings and omit markings more appropriate for in-depth study or miscue research. Figure 3–2 shows the miscue markings as a teacher would make them.

Marking Miscues

Substitutions, reversals, insertions, omissions, repetitions, and corrections are all common miscues frequently made by readers. Many teachers new to miscue analy-

Type of Miscue	Example of Marking	Miscue Marking Explained
Substitution	*gentle* This was the start of a grand voyage.	When readers say one word for another, mark the observed response above the expected response.
Reversal	**This was** Was this the end of his life …	When readers change the order of two or more words, write the words above the ER, or use a transposition sign.
Insertion	*^and* Bats make high beeping sounds.	When readers insert text, note it with a caret.
Omission	These sounds are too high- (pitched) for our ears.	When readers leave out text, circle the omission. If they omit an entire line, circle the line.
Complex Miscue	… watched newsreels of the *Hindenburg* explosion *listened to* and heard reports about it	When miscues occur together and there is not a way to see the word-for-word relationship, mark each miscue and bracket the sequence, indicating a complex miscue.

Figure 3–2. Miscue Marking Guide

sis try to consistently mark these miscues first. After they are comfortable with these, they can start marking more complex miscues.

Substitutions A word that a reader uses to replace the expected response is called a *substitution*. The miscue is written directly over the text item. Students who struggle with reading often use more substitutions than any other type of miscue. Matt read, "He had deducted his life to airships." Jennifer recorded:

201   *deducted*
He had dedicated his life to airships.

Jennifer recorded "deducted," the observed response, directly above the expected response, *dedicated*. Readers may substitute one or more words. For the following example, Matt read, "There was the start of a gentle voyage that would take them. . . ." Jennifer recorded:

103 This was the start of a grand voyage that would take them ....

(handwritten above: "There" above "This"; "gentle" above "grand")

In this sentence, Matt made a substitution for two words (*this* and *grand*). Jennifer marked each above the text.

Reversals   Reversals are a special kind of substitution in which the reader changes the order of two or more words. Reversals are marked by placing the observed response above the expected response or inserting the editor's transposition sign (⊓⊔). Matt read, "This was the end of his life. . . ." Jennifer recorded:

308 Was this the end of his life ....

(handwritten above: "This was" above "Was this")

Matt substituted "This was" for *Was this*. The miscue still sounds like language and does not significantly disrupt the meaning.

Insertions and omissions   When readers insert or omit text, the result is a miscue. Insertions are marked with a caret (^), while omissions are circled. Devon (a seventh grader) read: "Bats make high and beeping sounds. These sounds are too high for our ears." Jennifer recorded:

1002 Bats make high beeping sounds. These sounds are too

high pitched for our ears.

(handwritten: "and" inserted with caret between "high" and "beeping"; "pitched" circled as omission)

Devon inserted "and" while omitting *pitched*, yet the two miscues make sense in the context of the sentence.

Complex miscues   Sometimes students make miscues in such a way that teachers cannot see a word-for-word relationship. The entire sequence is marked as a complex miscue with a bracket. To decide if the miscue is complex, compare the observed response to the expected response. If you cannot separate the observed response into individual words, it is a complex miscue. Matt read, ". . . people around the world watched newsreels of the hydrogen explosion and listened to reports about it. " Jennifer recorded:

3001   ... people around the world watched newsreels of the ~~Hindenburg~~ *hydrogen*

explosion and ~~heard~~ *listened to* reports about it.

The complex miscue here is "listened to" for *heard*. Matt used "listened to" as a unit. He could not say "listened reports." Therefore the entire sequence is marked as a complex miscue with a bracket.

Markings That Concern Repetitions

Readers often use forms of repetition when they restate text, correct text, make unsuccessful attempts to correct text, or abandon a correct form. A line is placed under the repeated text and a circle is placed at the beginning of the repetition. Inside the circle is the letter or letters explaining the reason for the repetition. Noting these reading strategies gives the teacher important information about how the reader is monitoring for meaning and attempting to make the reading sound like language; this information may later be discussed in the RMA conversations. Figure 3–3 explains those markings that concern repetitions.

Repetitions (R)   Readers often repeat words and phrases when they come to an unknown structure and want to give themselves time to figure out something ahead in the line or to monitor for meaning. If the reader repeats, underline the amount of text that was repeated and place an *R* in a circle above the expected response. When Devon was reading *Aunt Flossie's Hats* (Howard 1995), he said, "Didn't come near our house on Center, Center Street, but we could hear fire engines racing down to St. Paul, Paul." Jennifer recorded:

1206   Didn't come near our house on ⓡ<u>Center</u> Street, but we could hear

fire engines racing down to St. ⓡ<u>Paul.</u>

Type of Miscue	Example of Marking	Marking Explained
Repetition	Didn't come near our house ⓡ on |Center Street	When readers repeat text, place an *R* in a circle above the word and underline the word for each repetition. *Center* was repeated once.
Correction	ⓒ was Aunt Flossie |has| so many hats!	When readers repeat to correct, underline the word and place a *C* in a circle above it.
Unsuccessful Attempt to Correct	ⓤⓒ ┌ther- ├thousands ├ther- ├thunderstorms There were|thunderstorms └ in the area	If a reader attempts to correct and is not successful, draw a line under the expected response to indicate repetition and mark a *UC* above.
Abandoning a Correct Form	… and gave Eckener a ⒶⒸ ┌ti-ker-type |ticker-tape parade in Manhattan.	If a reader abandons a correct response, place a line under it and put *AC* in a circle by the observed response.
Repetition That Affects More Than One Miscue	ⓒ ⓒ ⒶⒸ ⓒ race only And rice ⌒Only|the rich could afford	If a reader repeats and several things happen, record an empty circle at the beginning of the repetition and mark each miscue separately.
Repeated Miscue	ER: dirigible line 0601 deergable line 0703 dijible line 1102 derejible line 1106 dijible—RM	If a reader repeats the identical miscue on a single item, mark *RM* after each subsequent miscue.

Figure 3–3. Markings That Concern Repetitions

If the reader repeats the text multiple times, underline it as many times as he repeats it. Matt read, "Count Zeppelin, however, was a military man, military, military man at heart." Jennifer recorded:

0804   Count Zeppelin, however, was a military man at heart.

Corrections (C)   A correction occurs when the reader goes back to repair a miscue. It is marked by underlining the text and placing a C in a circle above the word. Devon read: "Aunt Flors was, has so many hats!" Jennifer recorded:

1009   Aunt Flossie has so many hats!

Devon corrected *has* for "was" but left "Flors" uncorrected. Notice that because Devon repeated, a line is placed under the expected response. However, his repetition was a correction, so the line is attached with the circled C. If Devon had continued to call Aunt Flossie "Aunt Flors," then Jennifer would put an RM (for repeated miscue) above the word every time he repeated it after the first time.

Repeated miscues (RM)   Repetition of a miscue for the same expected response is called a *repeated miscue*, and each is marked with an *RM* in a circle. There are three kinds of repeated miscues:

1. Substitutions or omissions that are identical. If Devon used "Flors" every time he encountered *Flossie* in the text or if he omitted it each time, Jennifer would mark RM each time after the first miscue.
2. Varied substitutions for the same ER. For the expected response *dirigible*, Matt read line 0601 as "deergable," line 0703 as "dijible," line 1102 as "derejible," and line 1106 as "dijible." Jennifer marked an *RM* only after the second "dijible," because it was an exact duplication of the earlier miscue on line 0703.
3. Substitutions and omissions that are function words are a special case. They are NOT marked with an *RM*. If Matt substituted or omitted the same function word (like *an, a, the, have, had, and, but*, or a preposition) more than once, Jennifer would mark it, but not add the *RM*. For example, if the ER was *this* and Matt said *that* each time, Jennifer would simply mark it as a substitution. The reason for this special case is that function words often signal different kinds of language relationships in each text occurrence.

Although marking repeated miscues might sound like a small detail, the information they provide to readers and teachers is large. Discussing repeated miscues in RMA conversations helps readers understand that they use placeholders (words that take the place of the ER and help them keep going in text) or that they make slight variations in text to come closer to their expected response. Note in Matt's *dirigible* example earlier that he worked with the sounds, trying to come closer to a word he might recognize. Talking about repeated miscues gives teachers and readers a new respect for how our brains work.

Unsuccessful attempt to correct (UC)   If a reader attempts to correct a miscue and still does not produce the expected response, a line is drawn under the word every time it is repeated. The teacher places a *UC* in a circle above the word to indicate that this is an unsuccessful attempt to correct. When Matt read, "There were thundersterms, ther-, thousands, ther- in the area, so it coursed south," Jennifer recorded:

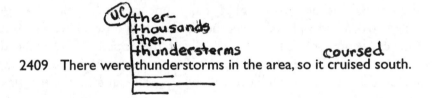

2409   There were thunderstorms in the area, so it cruised south.

Notice that Matt tried a word that looked quite similar, then tried to sound it out, resulting in a partial word (ther-). He then tried another similar-looking word and another partial word. He finally just continued. Jennifer placed a *UC* in a circle next to the last attempt.

Abandoning the correct form (AC)   Sometimes students read the correct form and then abandon it. The teacher marks an *AC* in a circle above the word, with a line under the word (indicating that the student repeated the word once). At one point in the miscue analysis, Matt read: ". . . and gave Eckener a ticker-tape, ti-ker-type parade in Manhattan." Jennifer recorded:

1108   ... and gave Eckener a ticker-tape parade in Manhattan.

At first Matt produced the expected word, but he thought he was wrong and changed it to a nonword. Notice that Jennifer marked a $ in front of the word to indicate it was a nonword.

26

Repetitions that affect more than one miscue   Occasionally a reader will make many miscues on a short section of text and it is difficult to see what is happening. Mark each miscue separately and underline the text that has been repeated. Place an empty circle above the line where the regression began. Teachers often write out what the student said in the margin of the paper. Matt read, "And only, only the rice could, race could afford to, the rich could only afford to travel by airship." Jennifer recorded what Matt said to the side and later went back to mark this miscue.

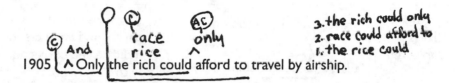

Many things occurred in this miscue. Matt corrected his insertion of "and" and corrected his substitutions of "rice" and "race" for *rich*. Eventually he produced a sentence that sounded like language and made sense. When there are many things occurring during a repetition, record what the reader says in the margins and return to mark more closely after the session is completed.

Additional Markings

Partial miscues and dialect are useful markings because they give the teacher important information on how readers correct and use language. Figure 3–4 shows how to use additional markings. We have omitted misarticulations, intonation shifts, and split syllables, because they are not generally focused on during RMA conversations. Goodman, Watson, and Burke (2005) provide information about how to use these markings.

Partials That Are Not Corrected

A *partial* is a miscue in which the reader does not complete the word. A dash (-) is placed behind the partial to mark it. Most often it is considered an omission if the reader leaves so little of the word that the teacher cannot tell what the word would have been. For example, Matt read, ". . . of putting several balloons inside a hollow, rig- structure." Jennifer recorded:

502   of putting several balloons inside a hollow rigid structure

Type of Miscue	Example of Marking	Miscue Marking Explained
Partial That Is Not Corrected	of putting several balloons inside *rig-* a hollow rigid structure	When a reader does not complete the word, use a dash (-) to indicate a partial. Listen for reader's rising inflection to identify partials.
Partial That Is Corrected	Travel over the ocean on ⓒ *pass-* a large passenger ship.	If a reader produces a partial and corrects it, indicate the correction with a ⓒ.
Dialect	ⓓ need to go to the hospital for emergency surgery	If a reader pronounces a word the way he or she does when speaking, place a circled *d* above it.

Figure 3–4. Other Markings

Note that she put the partial "rig-" directly over the expected response, *rigid.* Jennifer knew this was a partial because of Matt's rising intonation. His voice rose and he did not complete an entire word.

Partials that are corrected   Often readers make partial responses and then correct themselves. The teacher marks partials by placing a dash (-) after the word. Matt read: ". . . cheering widely as the han-, huge zeppelin flew, floated overhead." Jennifer recorded:

ⓒ *han-*   ⓒ *flew*
2003   ... cheering widely as the huge zeppelin floated overhead.

Matt corrected both miscues. The first is a partial, indicated by a dash (-) at the end of the word. Jennifer knew it was a partial because of Matt's rising intonation at the end of "han-."

Dialect   Dialect refers to the language variation of the reader. All language users have a dialect; it is the particular way their family or community pronounces words (like "pitcher" for *picture*), uses vocabulary (*pop* or *soda*), or forms syntactic variations ("be goin" for *was going*). Although we have included one example of a dialect miscue, Goodman, Watson, and Burke (1987, 2005) offer more detailed procedures for marking and coding them. If the reader makes a dialect miscue, the teacher marks a circled *d* on the typescript above the word in question and records the reader's response. For example, a student newly arrived in America from Great Britain read, "He'll need to go to hospital for emergency surgery." The teacher recorded:

126   He'll need to go to (the) hospital for emergency surgery.

The child omitted *the* because in England, *hospital* carries no article. So the teacher placed a *d* on the typescript to indicate the miscue was a dialectical preference and circled *the* to indicate an omission. Teachers who know their students well can generally tell if the miscue represents a mispronounced word or is a reflection of the student's dialect. Since everyone has a dialect, many teachers would not use dialect miscues as a focus of RMA conversations.

5. Conducting the Retelling

Unaided retelling   After Matt finished reading the story, Jennifer conducted a retelling. Miscue analysis *always* includes a retelling portion, since the teacher needs to know how well the reader comprehended the text. The retelling is student centered, so that the teacher can discover the meaning of the text as the reader constructs it, not in response to highly structured questions. After Matt completed the reading, Jennifer prompted, "Tell me in your own words what you remember about the story." She tape-recorded the retelling and made notes. As Matt retold the story, she used subtle body language (nodding, hand signals) that encouraged, "Go on, continue, tell me more." She was careful not to signal that a response was correct or incorrect.

Aided retelling   When Matt concluded, Jennifer asked him to tell her more about items he had already mentioned. She said, "You mentioned a boy in the story; tell me more about him." She was careful to use Matt's exact words. For example, Matt pronounced *Hindenburg* several different ways. Jennifer was careful to refer to it in the final way that Matt had used, "Hinderberg," when asking questions about it so that she would not distract him from what he remembered by substituting a new word. After she had exhausted everything that Matt had volunteered, Jennifer questioned more directly about the underlying story elements: "Tell me in a few words what the story was about," or "Sometimes writers have a lesson that they want us to take away. What do you think the lesson was in this story?" Then Jennifer asked Matt about details he omitted. Even though the session was tape-recorded, Jennifer made notes about the retelling to document Matt's tone of voice, gestures, frustrations, and so on. Many teachers create their own retelling guides, in which points are given for story elements or features of expository text. For example, for a narrative text retelling, the teacher would be listening for identification of key story characters, the setting, story problem, key story episodes, and problem resolution. Appendix E contains an example of a scoring protocol for narrative text, while Appendix F contains one for expository text.

6. Preparing the RMA Organizer

Note: The following procedure explains how teachers can code directly on the RMA organizer to prepare for the miscue conversation. This is a shortcut from the typical process, in which teachers mark and code the miscues on the same typescript and then select the miscues to complete an RMA (Goodman, Watson, and Burke 1987). Either way is appropriate to prepare for the RMA conversations.

After marking the typescript, Jennifer selected particular miscues for the RMA organizer. The RMA organizer is a form that offers a coding protocol for the teacher. It contains the text item, the miscue, and several questions regarding graphic similarity, syntactic and semantic acceptability, meaning change, and correction. These questions help teachers determine the relationship of the miscues to the systems of language, that is, how the reader uses semantic, syntactic, and graphic information, as conveyed through the miscues. It also prepares the teacher for the RMA conversation.

Jennifer consciously chose specific miscues that supported certain reading behaviors for Matt. As she listened to Matt read, she noticed that even though he had a great many miscues, he generally used the syntactic (grammar) system fairly effectively. His sentences sounded like language. He had more trouble with the semantic system. Matt tended to substitute words that looked similar to the text but did not make sense in the sentence. Jennifer wanted to start by pointing out Matt's strong reading strategies. She decided to begin with substitution miscues that did not change the meaning, because she wanted Matt to realize that some of his miscues were high level and did not need to be corrected. She showed him what he did well as a reader. Jennifer then moved to examples where he had corrected his miscues. Again, she was pointing out a strong reading strategy. Finally, because she wanted him to monitor his reading more closely, Jennifer discussed those miscues in which he had produced a nonword that looked similar to the text. At the end of this first session, Matt asked Jennifer for a copy of the transcript saying, "I didn't know I was that kind of reader. You know, a good reader." Figure 3–5 contains a portion of

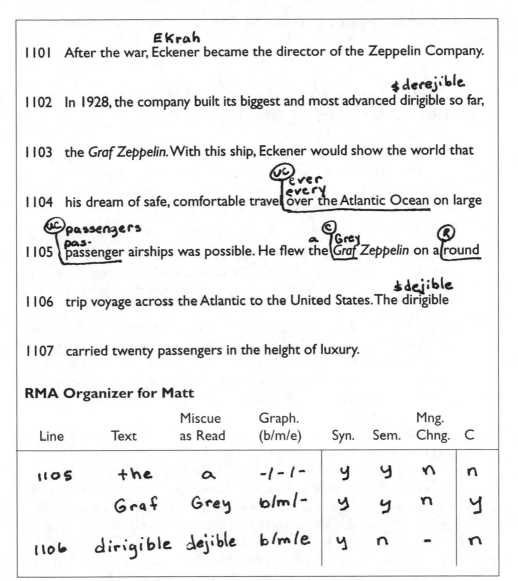

1101 After the war, Eckener became the director of the Zeppelin Company.
       (Ekrah)

1102 In 1928, the company built its biggest and most advanced dirigible so far,
       (＄derejible)

1103 the *Graf Zeppelin*. With this ship, Eckener would show the world that

1104 his dream of safe, comfortable travel over the Atlantic Ocean on large
       (UC) ever / every

1105 passenger airships was possible. He flew the *Graf Zeppelin* on a round
       (UC) passengers / pas-   *(a) (C) Grey*   *(R)*

1106 trip voyage across the Atlantic to the United States. The dirigible
       (＄dejible)

1107 carried twenty passengers in the height of luxury.

RMA Organizer for Matt

Line	Text	Miscue as Read	Graph. (b/m/e)	Syn.	Sem.	Mng. Chng.	C
1105	the	a	-/-/-	y	y	n	n
	Graf	Grey	b/m/-	y	y	n	y
1106	dirigible	dejible	b/m/e	y	n	-	n

Figure 3–5. Portion of Typescript and RMA Organizer for Matt

the typescript and the corresponding RMA session organizer for Matt. The following chapters explain the organizer in more detail.

Completing Matt's RMA Organizer

As Jennifer planned the RMA session for Matt, she needed to record selected miscues on the RMA organizer. Following is one miscue example ("a" for *the*).

We have described Jennifer's thinking as she filled in the RMA organizer (see Figure 3–5).

1105   ... He flew the *Graf Zeppelin* on a round

Jennifer read the sentence as Matt left it, with any other miscues corrected except the one in question. She also considered if the miscue may have been a dialect preference of Matt's. Then she completed the RMA session organizer. Jennifer's answers are in italics:

- Line: The numbered text line is noted. *1105*
- Text: This is the expected response. What was the original word? *the*
- Miscue as Read: This is the observed response. Write the miscue exactly as the reader last said it. *a*
- Graph. (b/m/e): Means graphophonic similarity. Does the miscue look like the expected response in the beginning (b), the middle (m), or at the end (e)? In the case of the miscue "a," no similarity is noted in the beginning, middle, or end to *the*, so Jennifer marked a *dash (-)* under each category. If the miscue is graphophonically similar at the beginning, middle, or end, mark it accordingly.
- Syn.: Means syntactically acceptable. To make this determination, Jennifer read the whole sentence as the reader left it, with all miscues corrected except the one in question. She asked, "Is the miscue syntactically acceptable within this sentence and the entire text?" To be syntactically acceptable, the miscue must sound like language and keep the grammar of the sentence consistent with the entire text. Since "a" sounds like language and is an article like *the* Jennifer marked y for yes.
- Sem.: Means semantically acceptable. This determination can be made only if the miscue is already syntactically acceptable. A miscue must sound like language in order to make sense. Since Jennifer had marked Matt's miscue as syntactically acceptable, she moved on to semantically acceptable. To decide if the miscue was semantically acceptable, Jennifer again read the whole sentence as the reader left it with everything corrected except the miscue in question. She asked, "Is the miscue semantically acceptable within this sentence and the entire text?" To be semantically acceptable, it must make sense. Since *a* and *the* are interchangeable in many cases, Jennifer marked y again.

- Mng. Chng.: Denotes meaning change. To make this determination, Jennifer read the sentence as the reader left it with all miscues corrected except the one in question. She asked, "Does the miscue change the meaning of the sentence in the selection?" Substituting "a" for *the* does not change the meaning, so Jennifer marked *n* for no.
- C: Means self-corrected. Was the miscue self-corrected? It wasn't, so Jennifer marked *n*.

Figure 3–5 shows the typescript and the RMA organizer for the "a" miscue, as well as three others.

As Jennifer selected miscues for the RMA session, she began to see patterns in Matt's reading behavior. She noticed that Matt produced a large number of substitutions (264 in the whole piece), of which 61 percent had high graphic similarity (similarity in at least two parts of the word). Examples of high graphic similarity miscues on one page of the typescript follow:

Text	Matt's Response
westward	westwhy (nonword)
dedicated	deducted
now	how
gigantic	gajent (nonword)
wanted	waited
Hindenburg	Hagenburg
unforgettable	unforgottable (nonword)

Looking at Matt's substitutions and his marked typescript, Jennifer knew that he was not always monitoring his reading. He used a combination of phonics knowledge and guesses based on the first and last letter of a word, making only a few self-corrections. Examining the RMA organizer, Jennifer realized that she needed to use RMA to do three things:

1. Help Matt revalue himself as a reader. His guesses, poor fluency, and few corrections informed Jennifer that he did not trust himself as a reader.
2. Have more conversations in which she could show him that some of his miscues did not change the meaning, so he could learn when to correct and when to keep going.
3. Teach Matt to use some other strategies besides sounding the word out or guessing based on the first consonant.

Chapter 7 discusses Matt's and Devon's work with RMA conversations.

Although this chapter highlighted completing an RMA organizer following miscue analysis, teachers using running record protocols can also use the RMA process. Often young children are assessed with running records; those miscues marked on the running record can also be transferred to an RMA organizer for RMA conversations. Appendix G contains an example of third grader Nathan's running record and corresponding RMA organizer.

Summing It Up and Moving On

This chapter explored how to conduct a miscue analysis and a retelling, then mark and prepare miscues for the RMA organizer. Matt's typescript segment (Figure 3–5) illustrates how Jennifer marked and coded his miscues. Reviewing the markings on the typescript and then transferring the miscues to the RMA organizer helped Jennifer decide on a productive focus for the RMA conversation. Chapter 4 examines how to use RMA as an assessment and instructional tool.

4

Using RMA as an Assessment and Instructional Tool

I know about a lot, but sometimes can't read the words that go with it.
—Dan, a High School Senior

This chapter will

- discuss the rationale behind RMA;
- highlight the protocol and procedures for implementing RMA sessions;
- examine RMA within the contexts of classroom reading routines; and
- offer procedures for documenting student progress and storing data.

RMA Informs Instruction

As an assessment and instructional tool, RMA is effective with elementary, middle, and secondary school readers, especially those who lack confidence in their reading abilities. By relying directly on individual or small-group responses to miscues, RMA sessions build comprehension, vocabulary, and fluency in readers. RMA embraces and empowers the voices of readers like Dan, an older reader who continually surprised Chris, his high school language arts teacher. During RMA conversations, Dan often gave accurate and detailed retellings, correctly using words he had mispronounced or skipped when reading aloud (Moore and Aspegren 2001). The opening quote shows how he once explained his reading challenge to Chris. Listening to Dan's retellings gave Chris insight into his spoken vocabulary, thus helping her plan instruction to increase vocabulary recognition in text.

As an assessment tool, RMA informs instruction. Karen, whose story is told in Chapter 5, often conducted minilessons outside of RMA sessions. These lessons focused on reading strategies that readers had discussed as effective during RMA sessions or strategies that Karen wanted them to try in order to increase their fluency and understanding. Chris, further introduced in Chapter 8, held reading conferences with her students using RMA strategies prior to having them meet in

CRMA groups. She based minilessons on the kinds of connections the readers made from their personal experiences to text, their difficulty with some tricky pronunciations and spellings, and their observations about the differences between fiction and nonfiction text.

RMA differs from traditional reading instruction in that readers examine oral reading substitutions, repetitions, omissions, insertions, and self-corrections, viewing them not as mistakes but as clues to what they were thinking about as they read. Sometimes miscues do not change the meaning of the text and sometimes they do. The idea is to reflectively consider and value patterns of miscues, and the thinking behind them, as a way for learners to understand the reading process.

Sometimes readers are fluent but lack comprehension. During RMA, they are encouraged to examine their unaided retellings, thus expanding their prediction and reasoning strategies and skills. For example, initially, Justin's retellings were brief and he did not want to add any details to them. Karen discovered that his vocabulary was growing and used that information to encourage deeper retellings, as seen in the following excerpt. The RMA group had finished listening to Justin's oral reading of a chapter in *Stone Fox* (Gardiner 1983) in which the main character relates the perils of a dangerous race. After discussing his miscues, the RMA group then listened to Justin's brief retelling, which Karen encouraged him to expand upon.

TEACHER: Justin, do you want to add any more to your retelling?
JUSTIN: No, I don't think so.
TEACHER: What does that word mean, *dangerous*?
JUSTIN: There were twists and turns in the road.
TEACHER: Good. So, how do you think little Willy felt about the ride?
JUSTIN: He was scared but he knew he had to keep going to win the race and help his grandpa keep his farm.

Sometimes retelling responses can be examined through the connections the reader is making to what is already familiar. Thomas, a fifth grader in Vicki's class, is learning to make thoughtful text-to-text connections. After listening to his taped reading and retelling during one RMA session, Thomas commented on the differences in how people wrote and spoke during the time of Paul Revere. (His retelling included his impressions of a portion of the text written as a letter in the story about Paul Revere.) He went on to make a connection to another text the class was reading about the explorers Lewis and Clark, saying, "People in the days of Paul Revere talked differently and spelled some words different than we do—just like some of the stuff we've been reading from Lewis and Clark."

Vicki commented: "I think the most important part of RMA for my students is the way we can make connections to self, text, and world." Applying prior knowledge and experiences to text is integral to both decoding and comprehension skills.

Readers use their knowledge of language cueing systems to make meaning from text. RMA conversations provide teachers and students with a better understanding of the reading process. For example, if a reader miscues on the word *home* by saying "horse," the meaning is altered but she has inserted a word that is syntactically the same part of speech—a noun—and looks similar to the original word. During RMA, the reader and teacher can discuss the reader's syntactic (grammatical) knowledge while also discussing her semantic (meaning-making) and graphophonic (sound-symbol) knowledge with a question such as "Why doesn't 'horse' make sense in that sentence? What word begins and ends like 'horse,' looks a little like it, but fits into the meaning of the sentence?" Chances are good the reader will self-correct such an obvious miscue before the question is even asked during RMA; however, that self-correction is also a valuable time to point out to the reader how her knowledge of language provoked the self-correction. Regardless, as RMA partners, the reader and the teacher share the instructional responsibility.

Organizing for RMA Instruction

RMA follows a series of steps that integrate the miscue procedure outlined in Chapter 3; these steps may be implemented into a classroom reading routine. The RMA process itself is flexible and should always respect the needs, abilities, and interests of the learner. And, although this book is primarily concerned with readers who struggle, we encourage teachers to also consider the process as a way of conducting reading instruction for all readers.

Step 1: Selecting Participants

RMA conversations can occur between the teacher and the student in a reading conference, between the teacher and a small group of students, or in collaborative reading groups (CRMA) assigned by the teacher in which students facilitate the conversation. Usually RMA groups are made up of three to four readers who vary somewhat in their reading abilities and characteristics. RMA conversations may also occur between the teacher and the student, as was the case with Dan, a high school senior, and Chris, his language arts teacher. Some participants may be fluent readers with low comprehension. Others, like Dan, may struggle with word recognition and fluency but may still be able to construct a reasonable degree of meaning from the text. RMA groups are not formed by arbitrary reading levels; rather, they are based on the teacher's decision about students who will work well together as they metacognitively explore (1) their high- and low-level reading miscues and (2) each group member's strategies for gaining meaning from text. The teacher is a member of the RMA group, participating as any other group member; however, there may be times when he must provide more sophisticated guidance in explaining the relationship of important miscues to language, learning, and the reading process.

Step 2: Gathering and Analyzing the Miscues

The miscue analysis, explained in Chapter 3, is the foundation for RMA as it reveals miscue and retelling patterns that help the teacher organize for RMA conversations. It provides effective record keeping for ongoing assessment of decoding strategies and comprehension, and it's far more effective and less expensive than working with published curriculum materials.

RMA begins with the miscue analysis. Administering and analyzing an oral reading and retelling is not required for *each* RMA conversation. For ongoing RMA conversations, it is necessary for teachers to mark only enough text to identify patterns of miscues that sustain conversations between and among learners. The results of a single miscue analysis can provide data for numerous RMA conversations since each audiotaped reading is played and discussed by the RMA participants. The retelling of the text is part of the RMA conversation, thus weaving fluency strategies with comprehension strategies. Readers discuss what they would change about the retelling to reflect greater accuracy and the kinds of learning connections they made to the text or that they can make to the text after listening to the taped retelling.

Step 3: Preparing the Miscues for RMA Discussion

There are two ways to prepare the miscues for RMA discussion. The first is less time-consuming for teachers and is more practical when conducting RMA with more than one group of readers; the second takes more time but is more appropriate when using RMA as classroom research to be shared formally with others. For example, Vicki and Chris plan to publish their findings about the use of RMA in the classroom, so they use the second option.

Option 1: Simplified RMA organizer In the first procedure, after coding the marked typescript and assessing the retelling, the teacher transfers the miscues to the miscue organizer, which includes the line of the text, the actual word in the text, the miscue as read, and a column to determine if the miscue (as the reader last read it) changed the meaning of the sentence. (Figure 4–1 provides a brief example and Appendix B provides a reproducible form.) The teacher then highlights or circles the miscues on the organizer that most clearly reveal the reader's attempts to make sense of the text or those that show high- or low-level decoding and compre-

Reader: _____

Date: _____

Name of Text: _____

Line of Text	Text	Miscue as Read/C	Did the miscue change the meaning?
_____	_____	_____	Yes No
_____	_____	_____	Yes No
_____	_____	_____	Yes No
_____	_____	_____	Yes No

Questions to think about:

- Does the miscue make sense?
- Does it change the meaning of the sentence?
- Why do you think the reader miscued?
- Why do you think the reader self-corrected?
- During the retelling, what connections to other text and life experiences did the reader make?

Some topics for discussion:

Figure 4–1. RMA Session Organizer 1: Simple

hension strategies. (If there is more than one RMA group, it is easier to circle the miscues and make copies.)

After completing the coding, the teacher jots down topics for discussion related to the reading and retelling that show the reader's use of decoding and comprehension strategies. Retelling discussions, especially, are sometimes difficult to jump-start; readers may not think they have anything to add to their retelling, or they may not notice things like consistently omitting the same word while reading the text but using it in the retelling. For example, Nathan, one of Karen's fourth-grade students, read a story about a beekeeper who made frames for the hives. Consistently, Nathan read "forms" for *frames*, but in the retelling, he talked about the beekeeper making frames. Having a set of topics to initiate the conversation is helpful to the teacher and the student so that revealing miscues like Nathan's do not go unnoticed. It is also helpful to include a few RMA questions on the RMA organizer to guide the teacher and the students who may be new to RMA. See Appendix B for a reproducible prototype. The teacher then gives each RMA participant a copy of the form as well as a copy of the marked typescript.

Option 2: Detailed RMA organizer   Teachers like Chris and Vicki, who plan to formally share RMA classroom research, may choose to transfer the miscues to a more detailed RMA organizer. See Appendix C for a reproducible copy and Chapter 3 for detailed instructions. Using this organizer helps teacher researchers reanalyze their initial data decisions while maintaining a clear, written record of reading response patterns. After transfer, the teacher highlights or circles the miscues to be discussed and gives a copy of the marked typescript to each RMA participant.

The line of the text, the actual text, and the miscue as read are represented on the organizer. As shown in a segment of the detailed organizer for Dan (Figure 4–2), the teacher records the graphic similarity of the miscue to the text at the beginning, middle, and end of the word. She also codes each miscue according to its syntactic (grammatical) and semantic (meaning) acceptability in the sentence. The teacher notes if the miscue changed the meaning of the sentence in the selection. Finally, self-corrections are noted on the form. Topics to discuss during the RMA conversations are drawn from a careful analysis of the decoding and comprehension strategies used by the reader and may be listed on the organizer. This detailed organizer is designed to more specifically focus on the reader's use of the language systems.

The teacher gives the readers a copy of the form showing the line, the text, and the miscue as read; there is no need to mark the language systems on the student copies. Having a copy of the organizer makes it easier for the readers to contribute to, and to follow, the RMA conversation. Depending on the age of the readers, the teacher may ask participants to fill in the graphic, syntactic, semantic, and self-correction columns after the RMA group has discussed the miscue's acceptability within the context of the sentence in which it was read.

Step 4: Laying the Ground Rules for RMA Discussions

Students must learn how to work in RMA groups, regardless of how the groups are configured or the age of the group members. The teacher establishes ground rules

Line	Text	Miscue as Read	Graph. (b/m/e)	Syn.	Sem.	Mng. Chng.	C
0101	Egyptian	E-ca-ble	b/–/–	n	–	–	n
0101	mummies	mammal	b/m/–	y	n	–	n
		mammy	b/m/–	y	n	–	n
0102	mummy	mammy	b/m/e	y	n	–	n
0102	find	follow	b/–/–	y	n	–	n
0102	mummies	mammals	b/m/–	y	n	–	n
0102	fascinating	fresh	b/–/–	y	n	–	n
0103	heard	heads	b/m/–	n	–	–	n

Topics for RMA conversation: possessive case, transition from mammy to mummy, using context clues, Egypt and Egyptian, searching, skipping, and moving on.

Figure 4–2. Detailed RMA Session Organizer for Dan

for discussion, communication, and cooperation and initially models RMA behaviors and language. Students sometimes want to say, "He messed up," or "That's not the right word," so careful monitoring and modeling by the teacher are required. The goal is for RMA participants to gradually realize that all miscues have meaning and to explore why the group member miscued rather than focus on the error. For example, Suzanne, one of Vicki's fifth-grade RMA students, consistently read "pirates" for *patriots* in a story about Paul Revere. The children had been participating in RMA for four weeks and were focusing less on pronunciation miscues and more on why the reader miscued. When the miscue was discussed, the other group members pointed out the graphophonic similarity between the words at the beginning, middle, and end as well as the idea that Suzanne might have been associating pirates with patriots because the text involved "people on two different sides. One side is the enemy, like pirates might be the enemy." They did agree that the miscue changed the meaning of the story, and once Suzanne understood the word, it was obvious she was relieved that finally, the text made sense!

Figure 4–3 offers some ground rules for RMA that we developed along with Karen, a Title I teacher.

Step 5: Conducting the RMA Session

The initial miscue reading session is audiotaped so that, during the RMA session that follows a day or two later, the group members can listen to the reading, view the marked miscues, discuss them, and add to the retelling. Either the teacher or a designated group member operates the tape player. On a rotating schedule, students listen silently to each of their partner's previously audiotaped miscue sessions and follow along on the marked typescript. The tape player is stopped

---

- Miscues are not to be called mistakes. Figure out what the reader was thinking when the miscue occurred.
- The person who is reading on the tape should be given the first chance to explain his or her miscue or retelling. Then others in the group may offer suggestions or ask questions to help figure out the miscue.
- Ask questions about the miscue: Does it make sense? Does it sound like language? What was the reader thinking about when the miscue occurred? Does it change the meaning? Did the reader self-correct?
- Be positive. Look for how that miscue helped the reader hold onto meaning.
- Use these words and phrases when you are having an RMA conversation: *placeholders, smart miscue, OK miscue, skip it and go on, repeated words, checking for meaning, take a running start, chunking the words,* and any other strategies we have learned in class.

Figure 4–3. Ground Rules for RMA

periodically as miscues marked for discussion occur. Other miscues not marked by the teacher may also be discussed if students wish to do so. When just beginning RMA, the teacher should start the discussion with a high-level, or "smart," miscue to provide participants with a sense of trust and motivation. After a few orientation sessions, students sometimes will notice revealing miscues that the teacher may have overlooked.

This is a flexible procedure that may be adapted to suit individual classroom schedules. The taped reading may not be finished in a single session but may extend into the next RMA conversation. As with reading groups, the RMA's session length and content depend on the readers. In general, RMA sessions last from ten to twenty minutes. A single miscue can yield rich discussions and exploration into vocabulary and meaningful connections to self and other texts. For example, there are times when the reader's mind picks up a word but the reader doesn't say that word until later in the text or during the retelling. When Nathan was working with Karen as a third-grade RMA participant, he substituted the word "gin" for *jar* throughout an entire story but in the retelling, to Karen's amazement, he talked about the character putting a flower in a jar of water.

During the RMA conversation, encourage the participants to think about whether the miscue made sense within the context of the sentence read and what the reader might have been thinking that prompted the miscue. Give readers the chance to explain their miscues, if they wish, and then ask for input from the other group members. Participants talk about high-level or "smart" miscues, which do not change the meaning of the text, or low-level (weak) miscues that significantly alter meaning. They explore how the reader is interpreting the text based on his or her background knowledge. For example, Nathan once read a story about a boy who stuttered without ever figuring out that the boy had a speech problem. He did, however, say during RMA, "I know he has a problem. Maybe he's short?" This was not unreasonable since the boy in the story was talking with a basketball coach.

The RMA conversation may turn to the types of reading strategies that were used to figure out the text. Readers then discuss a more productive strategy. Vicki is trying RMA with four puzzling readers: Suzanne, Thomas, Katie, and Rene. Rene reads fluently but retains little meaning. During one session, Rene noticed that several of her RMA group members made more miscues than she did but that their retellings were much more detailed than hers. Rene (who had made only one miscue) explained, "I think that the more miscues that you have, the better you understand what you read. I didn't have hardly any, and I couldn't tell what happened on the page." Rene is beginning to understand that she utilizes her knowledge of the graphophonic and syntactic cueing systems to read fluently but her semantic system is weak. She is not consistently monitoring for meaning; rather, she monitors primarily for fluency.

To aid RMA conversations, Vicki posts a chart with miscue markings and miscue terms such as *smart miscues, placeholders, substitutions, omissions, insertions, retellings,* and *repetitions*. She also includes reading strategies she has taught, such as making connections to text, thinking aloud, skipping and moving on, and chunking (looking for little words in big words). This chart helps focus the RMA discussions and gives readers specific vocabulary with which to talk about the reading process. Vicki reported that her struggling RMA group "caught on quickly" to the RMA process:

> By the third session, the readers came up with their own guidelines about how often to stop the tape and decided that one person would operate the tape player and the others would just signal. Now, we have met four times. They are getting very comfortable with one another and talk quite candidly about their miscues, using terms like *smart miscues, placeholders,* and *self-corrections*.

This is particularly useful as the students work from the coded typescript and select their own miscues for discussion. The group members also listen to the retelling and ask the reader if she would add or change anything. Other group members are then encouraged to comment. After that, the RMA process is repeated either by extending the listening and discussing to the next day or by beginning with the taped reading of another group member. The number and length of the sessions are dependent on the needs of the participants and the teacher's time and resources. The content of the discussion depends on the miscues selected for conversation as well as the age, interests, and abilities of the students.

Moving from RMA to CRMA

It is possible for students to function completely independently of their teacher, as shown in the work of Costello (1992, 1996). Older students, trained in miscue coding, may conduct their own miscue analyses without the teacher. They may then choose the miscues for collaborative retrospective miscue analysis (Costello 1992, 1996; Goodman and Flurkey 1996). There is some initial preparation involved, but learning miscue coding is no more complicated than learning organizational procedures associated with literature study groups or figuring out how to use peer editing marks for writing workshop. After an initial investment by the teacher, the students take ownership of the process.

Vicki's RMA group is now confident and competent enough with RMA procedures to move on to CRMA. As demonstrated earlier in this book and further explained in Chapter 6, CRMA gradually releases the responsibility for discussing miscues and retellings to the students. The teacher or the students may code the typescripts, but most importantly, the reading conversation is independently facilitated by the students in the group. (Specific steps for CRMA are detailed in Chapter 6.)

Chris, whom you will read more about in Chapter 8, moved among the CRMA groups in her classroom, listening in on conversations and documenting student comments. Sometimes she would offer her opinion on the reason for a miscue or suggest a connection the reader might make to the text to aid retelling. For struggling readers, especially, some initial experience in RMA with the teacher facilitating, choosing miscues for discussion, and participating in the conversation is recommended before moving on to CRMA.

Step 6: Documenting Student Progress and Storing Data

Since RMA is an assessment and instructional process, documentation is important to track the reader's progress. The following procedures will yield excellent data and make record keeping much more valid and useful:

1. Give the Burke Reading Interview and a reading interest inventory (see Chapter 2 for more information on the Burke Interview and Appendix A for Burke Interview questions). You can make up your own interest inventory or use a published one.
2. After the first miscue session, set no more than three reading goals with each student. Review them regularly with the students, update their progress, and change the goals as needed. In addition to reader goals, include predetermined reading curriculum goals and benchmarks.
3. Keep the marked typescripts and retelling guides in a binder or folder in chronological order. Maintain a folder for each student.
4. Create a chart for recording the percentage of comprehension for each retelling. This gives a quick overview to share with parents and the principal, as well as with the reader. (See Appendices E and F for reproducible retelling guides.)
5. Ask students to keep a list for a week of all the things they read and write. This will surprise them. At the end of three or four months, repeat the procedure.
6. Ask each student to keep a list of books read for recreation as well as in-class reading. Ask students to write a one- or two-line summary recommending (or not) each book to a friend or a teacher. This will help you document how the RMA process has influenced reading behaviors in general. With high school students, the teacher may want to develop a chart of different reading genres on which the class can keep track of their reading in general.

7. Give the Burke Reading Interview again after three to four months and discuss changes in responses with the reader. Ask the reader to complete another reading interest inventory. It is surprising how interests expand as a result of RMA conversations with others.

8. Ask students to individually evaluate the RMA process: what is going well and what is not. Do this periodically to troubleshoot any problems.

9. As you participate in RMA or observe during CRMA, keep a set of white labels or sticky notes handy. When you hear something insightful or revealing, write it down, date it, and put it in the reader's folder.

10. At the end of your typical grading period, review each student's folder. Determine progress in fluency, decoding, comprehension, and confidence. Mark the benchmarks for your curriculum goals according to how well the reader has met them. You will be pleasantly surprised.

Summing It Up and Moving On

This chapter introduces the reader to the RMA process for helping students critically examine their oral reading miscues and interpretations of text. The steps are (1) select the RMA participants, (2) conduct the miscue analysis and retelling, (3) prepare the miscues for the RMA session, (4) lay the ground rules for communication during the first RMA session, (5) conduct the session, and (6) secure and store the data from each session, reviewing it regularly for patterns of reader response or changes in reading progress.

Teachers find that RMA lends a new dimension to the development of reading as a meaning-making process for struggling readers. In the next chapter, we discuss patterns of reading that emerged from RMA conversations with three fourth-grade boys in a Title I reading classroom. These patterns informed and guided the RMA process.

5

Reflecting on Patterns of Reader Response in a Title I Reading Classroom

What do you think was going on in your brain when you read that?
—Karen, Title I Reading Specialist

This chapter will

- explore patterns in reading and reading response in ten RMA conversations;
- examine the difference between high- and low-level miscues in various contexts;
- demonstrate the power of reflective response to reading miscues in building confidence, empowerment, vocabulary, and comprehension among struggling readers; and
- demonstrate reading gains and changes in perceptions of reading.

Exploring Patterns in Reading and Reading Response

We often wonder what goes on in the minds of readers who struggle no matter what we do to try to reach them. This chapter documents patterns of RMA response from three struggling readers who were a puzzle to their classroom teachers. Through RMA conversations, the students learned to distinguish high-level miscues (those that *do not* appreciably change the meaning of the sentence in which they are read) from low-level miscues (those that *do* alter the meaning of the sentence in which they are read). The boys learned to view themselves as good readers and to choose effective reading strategies that they may never before have considered. RMA conversations about reading miscues suggest patterns of reading strategies that may either positively or negatively affect the learner's reading progress and perceptions of reading. Finding and reflecting on these patterns can inform instructional decisions.

Getting Started

Karen, a Title I reading teacher, was no stranger to miscue analysis or to RMA. She and Rita had conducted an earlier six-month study with Nathan as a third grader. He became a leader in the new fourth-grade RMA group, composed of Nathan, Justin, and Steve. Rita and Karen designed the second study.

As previously detailed, prior to the RMA process, Karen administered a Burke Reading Interview (Burke 1987) to each of the children (see Appendix A). She conducted a miscue analysis and transferred miscues from the marked typescript and her retelling notes to an RMA session organizer. The miscues focused the follow-up RMA session, but the conversation was not limited to them. (See Appendix B for a blank simple organizer.)

At the beginning of the RMA session, Karen gave each boy a copy of the marked typescript. Rita was there to observe for research purposes. Karen and Rita explained the miscue marking system to the boys and reviewed the difference between smart miscues and OK miscues—that is, smart miscues do not alter the meaning of the sentence in which the miscue is read (Y. Goodman 1996) and OK miscues might alter the meaning but result from an attempt to make sense of the text. During one RMA session as a third grader, Nathan actually coined the phrase *OK miscue* when he explained, "It's an OK miscue. It changed the meaning a little but it helped me keep on reading" (Moore and Brantingham 2003, 473).

With the marked typescript in front of them, the group listened to the tape of the reading until either the teacher or one of the boys wanted to discuss a miscue. They also listened to the retelling. The session usually lasted about thirty minutes.

No miscue was ever considered a total loss. Justin and Steve, at first, wanted to call the miscues "mistakes" or say, "He messed up." Prior to each of the early RMA sessions, Karen emphasized (1) that every miscue is an attempt to make meaning and (2) that group communication rules required participants to first listen to what the reader had to say about his miscue before offering their own comments. To discuss miscues, Karen stopped the tape player and initiated a conversation with questions such as "Did the miscue make sense?" and "What do you think _____ [name of the reader] was thinking when he miscued here?"

Karen encouraged the boys to take turns discussing (1) the reasoning behind the miscues, (2) interesting or challenging vocabulary words, (3) the meaning of the text captured in the retelling, and (4) patterns of miscues in their own reading and that of the other participants. It took time for the process to evolve, but eventually, rich discussions about words and textual meaning distinguished the RMA conversations. Often, as the reader listened to the miscues he had made while reading, he automatically corrected many high-level and low-level miscues. The boys enjoyed discovering patterns of miscues and strategies used, such as substitution of placeholders to maintain meaning. And as the boys became better readers, their retellings were much more complete and the retelling portion of the RMA conversation became a time for them to make connections to the text.

Documenting Patterns in Reader Response

Research in language development shows that children learn by sound-symbol pattern recognition—information that is particularly informative in the design of reading instruction (Moustafa 1997). To determine miscue patterns, Karen checked the graphophonic similarity of each miscue from the initial miscue analysis against the actual text and decided whether or not the miscue was syntactically or semantically acceptable within the context of the sentence. She also listed self-corrections. By way of quick review: to be graphophonically similar, the word has to have similar graphic and corresponding sound features; syntactically acceptable miscues are associated with the grammar of the language; semantically acceptable miscues refer to meaning.

By exploring these patterns, Karen better understood pronunciation choices as well as how each reader constructed meaning from text. Later, in the RMA conversation, she was able to more authentically convey that information to the readers. For example, a strategy common to all three readers was repetition, or checking the text by rereading. When the group discussed this, Justin and Steve said they thought rereading was a mark of a poor reader instead of a strategy used by strong readers to confirm text and meaning.

In the rest of this chapter, selected transcribed excerpts from ten consecutive RMA sessions show how miscue patterns demonstrate the growing abilities of Nathan, Justin, and Steve to (1) trust their self-corrections, (2) value themselves as readers, (3) understand substitution as part of the developing reading process, (4) develop word-solving strategies through connections to text and prediction, (5) critically rethink the text and develop stronger vocabulary, and (6) learn more about themselves as readers.

Learning from Self-Corrections

The first RMA conversation centers on the use of self-corrections. It also highlights teacher interference in the RMA conversation. (Karen aptly calls such interference a "teaching miscue.") Nathan was reading from the book *Frindle* (Clements 1996). On the tape, Nathan self-corrected his partial pronunciation of the word *served*.

0002   She knew Mr. and Mrs. Allen because they had served together on

0003   the building committee when the old Lincoln School was torn down and

0004   the new one was built six years ago.

49

During the RMA conversation Karen asked Nathan to explain why he self-corrected. Smiling, Nathan said, "Because it didn't sound right." Just as important, the self-correction of *served* prompted a review of the chapter and a strategic conversation about *blueprint*, a word none of the boys had understood prior to this:

JUSTIN: *Served* means working together, like a committee.
NATHAN: Doesn't that mean like a group of people?
TEACHER: Yes, good connections.
STEVE: Does that mean they sat down to talk about the blueprint we read about before—the committee probably designed the building.
NATHAN: Yeah, probably put it on construction paper.
ALL: (*Together*) The blueprint!

RMA is a fluid process that empowers students to take the conversation in directions meaningful to them. During this session, Karen planned to center the conversation around self-corrections and the way readers know how to self-correct based on their knowledge of language. While that was accomplished, Karen also observed the students solving words based on context clues and their own personal connections to text.

The group discussed another self-correction miscue: during a repetition of the last line, Nathan corrected "caffeine" to *coffee*.

0020   and Nick sat on the rocking chair that faced Mrs. Chatham across the

0021 coffee table.

Nathan read, ". . . Mrs. Chatham across the coo-, caffeine, coffee table." Justin motioned to stop the tape and Nathan was given the opportunity to explain his thinking behind the miscue. Interestingly, this revealing miscue was one Karen had overlooked for RMA discussion.

JUSTIN: He said "caffeine."
NATHAN: (*Proudly*) I changed it.
TEACHER: What happened when you changed it? Do you know what's in coffee?
NATHAN: Yeah, caffeine!
TEACHER: What kind of miscue is that?

JUSTIN: I think he was kind of turning the word inside out to get it.
NATHAN: It's a smart miscue.

Viewing this miscue from the influence of prior knowledge on readers striving to make meaning provided a springboard into an RMA discussion that clearly showed the reading process at work. Sometimes, however, teachers become too focused on their own agendas, overlooking what the reader has to say. It is obvious in the "caffeine" for *coffee* example that the teacher wanted Nathan to say it was an OK miscue, a meaningful placeholder, while working on pulling a definition from him. As Karen said, "The heart of RMA is that the child tells us what [he] think[s] rather than the teacher giving the explanation."

"He's a Good Reader": Revaluing the Reader

Justin is the reader in the next selection. The audiotape had captured the expression and enthusiasm with which Justin read Chapter 10 of *Frindle* (Clements 1996). His appropriate use of placeholders (substitutions) as well as his new confidence in word solving shone.

0001   Mrs. Fred, the school secretary, looked up and smiled. "May I help

you?"

Karen stopped the tape to inquire about this interesting miscue, which Justin both explained and self-corrected.

TEACHER: Justin, tell us what you were thinking about when you said "security."
JUSTIN: It's secretary . . . the secretary is kind of in charge, like a security guard.
TEACHER: And do the words look and sound kind of alike?
NATHAN: Yep.

Justin was working hard at making sense of text. His substitutions followed by self-corrections indicated that he was engaged in the meaning of the story. His confidence as a reader was increasing. After discussing most of Justin's miscues that day as "good" reading strategies, Nathan commented emphatically, "He's a *good* reader."

Seeing Through the Mind's Eye: Substitutions Reveal the Reading Process

There are times when the reader's mind picks up a word but the reader doesn't say the word until later in the text (Watson 1996a). For example, in the fourth RMA session, when listening to Nathan read *Frindle* (Clements 1996), it was evident he used the substitution strategy while his mind considered the actual word. This is an interesting pattern of response often observed in readers whose comprehension belies oral reading fluency. Early in the text, Nathan read "broadly nodded" instead of *barely noticed,* but much later in the text he said the word "notice" instead of what was written in the text.

0011   People in Westfield ~~barely noticed it~~ (broadly nodded ®) anymore.

0019   ...and paper and ~~dozens~~ (notice) of other items.

TEACHER: Let's turn off the tape a minute. I want to show you something that Nathan's brain is doing when he reads. See how he said "broadly nodded" here?

STEVE: It's *noticed.*

TEACHER: Yes, but let's look here and see where later he uses the word *notice.* What do you think is happening, Nathan?

NATHAN: I wasn't sure . . .

JUSTIN: He saw it before.

TEACHER: What do you think was going on in your brain when you read that?

NATHAN: (*Pauses and studies the text*)

The teacher's questions guided Nathan's understanding of the reading process to a conscious level. Although these are still low-level miscues, it is evident that at some point Nathan realized the word *notice* and slipped it into the text he was reading.

The next example is similar but it shows connections to other words previously read and discussed in the text. Nathan read:

0009   Then it became a habit.

0030   Her poster about the ~~forbidden~~ (harking habit) word

Nathan read "habit" one page prior to where he inserted "habit" for *word* in the phrase *forbidden word*. By examining this miscue and others like it, we learned that this is how Nathan's mind worked: he picked up a word earlier in the text and later inserted it elsewhere where it usually made sense. We are not sure why Nathan read "harking," but, syntactically, "habit" works in this phrase since saying the word *Frindle* is "forbidden" in the book *Frindle*. The children in the story ignore the mandate, and eventually saying the word becomes a habit at their school. In the following conversation, the teacher points out the complexity of the language and thinking process in the RMA conversation and Nathan affirms what happened:

TEACHER: Now look here (*motions for the boys to all look at her text*). He read "habit," and later, here (*pointing to typescript*), what does he say?
STEVE: "Habit"! It makes sense, but not "harking."
TEACHER: What does *forbidden* mean?
JUSTIN: Can't do it . . . might get into trouble.
TEACHER: Yes, was the forbidden word now becoming a habit?
NATHAN: That's what I thought!

The readers were fascinated by the way Nathan created meaning from word associations as he read. He stored words in his mind for later use that he had not yet read aloud or needed. Indeed, this was truly a window on the reading process (Goodman 1973; Y. Goodman 1996). When complex concepts are involved, scaffolding instruction (Vygotsky 1978), or guiding the reader toward greater meaning during RMA, is often necessary.

Substitutions came in many forms. They were omissions, nonwords, or words that were graphophonically similar to the actual text. Helping the readers understand that some kind of rationale or meaning informed substituting one word for another took some time. Some examples of the discussion about levels of substitution follow. Nathan was the reader.

                                        snarfed

0008 Searchlight barked and snarled and jumped at

            closer

0009 the closed door.

Karen stopped the tape player at Steve's request. He began the following conversation:

STEVE: He said "snarfed."
JUSTIN: It's *snarled* . . .

TEACHER: Nathan, what do you think of when you hear the word *snarled*?

NATHAN: Mean, dangerous, a dog.

TEACHER: Nathan read "snarfed"! How did that sound to you?

JUSTIN: Like a growl . . .

TEACHER: He said a word kind of like *snarled* sounds, right?

NATHAN: (*Breaking in*) It was a smart miscue. It meant the same. I mean, a dog can sound like that, like "snarfed." Is it a real word?

TEACHER: Did it change the meaning of the sentence?

NATHAN: A little. Maybe it's more like an OK miscue . . . but I like the sound.

JUSTIN: Someone might not know what "snarfed" means . . .

TEACHER: Yes, it's not a real word, but it is a placeholder and a good one that let him keep going. That's the smart part.

While "snarfed" or the use of a nonword is not a high-level miscue, it was important not to devalue Nathan's line of reasoning; one of the ground rules of RMA is to recognize that every miscue has meaning. To have classified "snarfed" as a weak miscue or mistake without meaning would have undermined the confidence and learner empowerment established thus far. What may sound like a teacher *cheerleading* gives the reader the confidence to explain without the fear of being corrected in front of peers. Asking readers to think about a miscue in relation to the connections they are making to their experience and knowledge ("snarfed" was an animal sound to Nathan) revalues readers and reading while gaining understanding and trust among RMA members.

Information coming from the RMA session informs instruction. The RMA conversation should explore all options related to the reader's miscues or understanding of meaning, thus guiding instructional decision making. Readers like Nathan may have relied heavily on graphophonic clues since they first began to read. When they become aware of different strategies, they must be allowed time to practice them and think about how the new strategies support their reading.

In another miscue reading, Justin substituted "samyods" for *samoyeds* to identify the dogs in *Stone Fox* (Gardiner 1983). Later, during the RMA conversation, he explained this as a strategy that helped him "keep going." Through these examples and conversations, the readers discovered it is possible to maintain meaning without always accurately pronouncing important words and without knowing the precise meaning of some less important words.

Making Connections to Text

To bring out each learner's meaning-making strategies, Karen often asked what they were thinking about as they read or retold a story. In a retelling miscue session, Justin introduced the word *interrogated*, then proceeded to accurately describe the meaning. Justin's list of new words grew to include advanced vocabulary such as *treacherous*, *consumer*, and *enchanted*. After only a few RMA sessions, Justin's rapidly developing vocabulary was evident. When Karen asked him to describe what *interrogated* meant in *Stone Fox* (Gardiner 1983), Justin said that it meant "being questioned a lot."

In the RMA discussion a week later, there was another interesting conversation between Justin and Karen about the word *treacherous*, again demonstrating patterns in Justin's vocabulary gains.

TEACHER: When they were on their way to Doc Smith's to get the medi-
cine . . . tell me about that ride.
JUSTIN: It was . . . um . . . (*looks back in his copy for the word*) "treacherous."
TEACHER: What does that mean, *treacherous*?
JUSTIN: Bumpy and scary, sort of.

Personal style and interpretation of text are rich resources for RMA. After viewing the videotapes of the ten RMA sessions, it was apparent that Steve was very discreet about how and when he contributed to the conversation. His RMA response to one of the lines from Nathan's taped reading helped Karen better understand Steve. Nathan read the following line, repeating "trust fund."

21   The checks that went into Nick's trust fund got bigger and bigger.

NATHAN: What's a trust fund?
TEACHER: Do you know what a fund is?
JUSTIN: No . . .
TEACHER: What do you think your parents try to save money for?
JUSTIN: Things to buy . . . like for the house.
NATHAN: Food.
STEVE: They could be used for college only.
TEACHER: Let's think about where we could find out about funds if Steve
hadn't told us.

After listening to the other two boys grapple with the term *trust funds*, Steve seriously explained they could be used only "for college." Justin and Nathan seemed surprised. This provoked a discussion about how not all readers have experiences or connections that unravel meaning; therefore, the next strategy is to seek a knowledgeable other or a reference resource.

Using Prediction Strategies

Prediction strategies can be strengthened by conversations about syntax that draw from the reader's natural understanding of grammar. The teacher may ask, "What word fits here? How do you know?" In one RMA session, Steve discussed the miscue of "no" for *none*, saying that the word did not quite "fit" but since they were both "no" words, it made sense—an example of an OK miscue. In another example, Justin read "dangers, twists, and turns" for *dangerous twists and turns* (Gardiner 1983, 70) and the group decided Justin's version was a better indicator of what lay ahead for the character Little Willy of *Stone Fox*. Neither boy's miscues significantly altered the meaning, so the conversations focused on how they used their knowledge of syntax to predict and convey meaning.

Critically Rethinking the Text

During the fifth RMA session, the group listened to a tape of Steve reading aloud from *Stone Fox* (Gardiner 1983). His reconstruction of text (note the insertions in lines 0010 and 0012) did not change the meaning, and later Karen learned that Steve's "Timon" miscue went unnoticed because none of the boys had ever heard of the Teton Mountains. One significant miscue, however, led to a rich discussion:

0010 farmhouse. ^and ^the The roof was covered with freshly fallen false

0011 snow. A trail of smoke escaped from the stone

0012 chimney. ^and ^the The jagged peaks of the Teton Timon Mountains shot up in the

background.

0013 toward the clear blue sky overhead. "Yes, sir," he remembered

Grandfather

0014 saying. "There are some things was in this world worth dying for." days

At line 0014, Nathan enthusiastically waved for Karen to stop the tape. The following conversation took place.

TEACHER: He said, "There was some days in this world worth dying for." Does that make sense?

JUSTIN: There *are* some things . . .

NATHAN: Kind of . . .

STEVE: It sort of balanced out . . .

TEACHER: Balanced out?

STEVE: He might live?

JUSTIN: (*Rereads the line aloud*)

STEVE: There's some stuff that's so important . . .

NATHAN: (*Finishes*) That you can die for it!! You'll do anything for it.

This conversation revealed the growing facility of the boys to critically re-think a text for greater meaning as RMA partners. It also showed their developing skill in metacognitive conversation in which they shared the meaning-making process with each other. This is often difficult for young readers (Davenport 2002). This conversation also demonstrated their developing awareness of the value of group collaboration to solve and interpret text.

In addition to gaining greater meaning, the boys were learning how good readers often rely on their knowledge of syntax and conventional cues. Steve's taped reading continued, opening an insightful window onto the reading process.

0037   Searchlight pulled the sled down Main Street

0038   past the crowd. Little Willy saw Miss Williams, his teacher, and

Mr. Foster from

0039   the bank and Hank from the post office. And there were Doc Smith

0040   and Mayor Smiley and Dusty the drunk. The city

0041   slickers were there. And even Clifford Snyder, the . . .

During the RMA conversation, Karen drew the students' attention to Steve's "rewriting" of text following his own line of prediction. Here is how the conversation went:

TEACHER: Steve, look one line up where you said, "and the Mayor."

JUSTIN: *(Jumping in before Steve can answer)* Oh, I know what he could've done. He could've just went right there and came right back up and reread it *(referring to a fix-up strategy introduced in class by Karen).*

NATHAN: Mayor? Oh, mayor! He said "and the mayor." He added a word but it wasn't even there.

TEACHER: Well, listen to what he said and tell me why you think he said it. This is how Steve said it, "And there were Doc Smith and the mayor smiling and Dusty the drunk."

NATHAN: . . . Smelling!

STEVE: No, it is not. I added "the."

TEACHER: You added "the," and what else did you do?

STEVE: *(Confused, he starts to reread what he has just heard himself read on tape.)*

TEACHER: And look at "the mayor." You said, "and the mayor smiling."

STEVE: Mayor?

TEACHER: Why do you think you said "smiling"? There're some good clues in the word. If you look at how the author wrote the word, there's a clue for you.

STEVE: Maybe that's his name!!

STEVE AND JUSTIN: Mayor Smiley . . .

STEVE: That's his name!

JUSTIN: Yeah, his name.

NATHAN: I thought it must be his last name.

TEACHER: Steve added the word "the" and said, "the mayor smiling." Did it make sense?

NATHAN: Like they are smiling. And that's his name, too.

STEVE: *(Excited)* Why do we need to know his name? As long as we know he's the mayor!

NATHAN: Yeah . . . you don't know their name but you know it's a person.

This particular miscue represented an important lesson in valuing how readers interpret and change text based on their predictions. The miscue originated with Steve, who momentarily withdrew from the RMA conversation to reread the text, then stepped back in with new information. His miscue is complex in that he interprets the mayor's name as a description of the man and immediately translates that knowledge into his own rewriting of the text. And, in the end, his miscue really did not change the meaning; in fact, it illuminated it to a certain extent. This RMA session demonstrated to Steve how he was predicting and constructing meaning *as* he read, which was a breakthrough. Steve's confidence soared and he showed one of his rare smiles.

Empowering Students

Strategies like placeholders and substitutions empowered the readers to move on with their reading or sometimes to realize that their choices were high-level miscues. For example, referring to a miscue discussed earlier in the chapter, Nathan said he substituted "broadly nodded" even though he "knew it didn't make sense but it sounded OK; then [he] could figure it out later." And he did.

During the final RMA conversation, Justin was the reader but he had made only one high-level miscue. He was reading *Charlotte's Web* (White 1952). Once quiet and shy, Justin had become much more verbal during the RMA sessions. In this conversation, he took charge of interpreting his own miscues and reading strategies.

Obler

0009 Mrs. Arable gave him a feeding around noontime each day, when

Fern was

0010 away in school.

JUSTIN:	I wasn't sure what her name was . . . so I made it up.
TEACHER:	So you used a placeholder . . . that's good. Nathan does that a lot, too.

It should be noted that after twice using the placeholder, Justin was able to solve the word midway through the text. At the end of the RMA session, Nathan, who considered himself the RMA expert of the group, looked at Karen and commented, "He's *really* a good reader now."

In his last miscue session with Karen, Justin discussed the word *enchanted*—found in both *Charlotte's Web* (White 1952) and *Harry Potter and the Sorcerer's Stone* (Rowling 1998)—saying that "it means something different" in *Charlotte's Web*. Justin explained, "In *Harry Potter*, it's like magic, but in *Charlotte's Web*, Wilber is a great pig—he dug a tunnel to keep the baby warm. She felt happy . . . enchanted." He later shared that information in the final RMA session:

TEACHER: What did you think of the author's use of the word *enchanted* there?

JUSTIN: She was shocked, excited.

TEACHER: Would you have used that word?

JUSTIN: No, I'd think of another word . . . it's sort of different in *Harry Potter*. It's magic in *Harry Potter*, but here, Fern feels happy or something because her baby is safe.

Justin had truly become an empowered reader. Prior to the RMA conversations, he rarely made text-to-text connections.

In the final RMA session, Karen noticed the youngsters discussed the reading process almost exclusively through miscue terminology. Justin self-corrected each miscue and, later, the boys discussed them.

0032   Wilbur was poking the straw with his snout. In a short time

0033   he had dug a tunnel in the straw. He crawled into the tunnel and

disappeared from sight,

0034   completely covered with straw. Fern was enchanted. It relieved her

0035   mind to know that her baby would sleep covered up,

The resulting RMA conversation clearly represents reader empowerment framed by the other readers' knowledge of the strategies of self-correction, smart miscues, and repetition.

NATHAN: He said "porking" then "poking."

STEVE: It's about a pig . . .

TEACHER: What do you notice Justin doing a lot?

NATHAN: Smart miscues. Self-corrections, too.

TEACHER: What about those with the underline and R on top?

NATHAN: It's right! He's making sure . . .

TEACHER: Sort of! He's repeating to be sure. We know how important repetition can be. How did you know what *enchanted* meant?

JUSTIN: I read it before in my Harry Potter book Dr. Moore gave me.

TEACHER: Do you know what a snout is? We've not talked about that word.

JUSTIN: Pig's nose.

TEACHER: I liked your "porking" miscue. What does pork make you think of?

JUSTIN: I self-corrected it.

NATHAN: A pig.

STEVE: A porker!

Reading Perceptions

Karen was interested in how RMA affects student perceptions of the reading process. She administered the Burke Reading Interview (Burke 1987) with each student prior to the first RMA session and again after the last one. At the beginning of the RMA sessions, each reader indicated he considered reading to be "sounding it out." To get help with a word, each reader would "ask the teacher" or "look it up in the dictionary." People the boys considered good readers were either their teacher or their parents.

After the final RMA conversation, Steve considered reading as "making sense" of the book, and Nathan said reading was "making smart and OK miscues" to figure out what the book said. Each of the boys said they used strategies such as "placeholders," "getting a running start," "looking for small words in big words," and "reading on to get more meaning." They all considered themselves good readers.

As far as individual progress is concerned, Justin went from being labeled a struggling reader who was targeted for special education services to a confident, competent reader. His classroom grade in reading jumped from an F in October to a high B in April. Justin made clever text-to-text connections (Keene and Zimmermann 1997) as his vocabulary soared.

Besides obvious gains in reading comprehension, Nathan assumed a leadership role. He was supportive of Justin and Steve, helping them view their miscues as smart or OK. During the RMA conversations, unlike in the classroom, the hallway, the lunchroom, and the gym, Nathan was not labeled a troublemaker.

He was empowered to give his opinions responsibly and to serve as an RMA expert on occasion.

Steve's vocabulary increased, but his ability to analyze and synthesize miscues and, later, predict text was most impressive. He often went beyond the other two participants in imagining the rationale behind his miscues. Behind Steve's words were a thousand other thoughts that sometimes emerged as personal connections to the text. For example, during the RMA discussions of *Stone Fox* (Gardiner 1983), Steve connected to the trials of the boy in the story, sometimes explicating Little Willy's feelings and fears for the others. Karen learned to be patient with this reader whose every comment seemed to stem from thoughtful, sometimes lengthy consideration.

Documenting Reading Gains and Losses

In addition to recording reading gains and losses, teachers should also document observations and anecdotes. With that in mind, Karen chose to compare her students' accuracy in retelling during the first miscue analysis with the final miscue retelling. She created informal retelling guides fashioned after those of Bill Harp (2000) to derive percentages based on the number of details expected in the retelling versus the number the reader mentioned. See Appendices E and F for the retelling guides.

Figure 5–1 shows that Justin made the highest gains, going from a 60 percent on the first retelling to a 97 percent on the last. While the retelling represents only answers from a simple guide, it is an accurate documentation of one way of assessing reading ability. Nathan did not score as high as the other two boys; however, in the previous year his score increased from an instructional level of preprimer on the *Qualitative Reading Inventory* (Leslie and Caldwell 1988) to second-grade instructional level after six months of RMA with Karen.

	October	April
Nathan	70%	80%
Justin	60%	97%
Steve	75%	90%

Figure 5–1. Reading Gains from October to April for Nathan, Justin, and Steve

Summing It Up and Moving On

A reader's responses to text, whether in the context of miscues or retellings, may not typically be realized as examples of the reader's attempt to create meaning. RMA gives the teacher a valuable glimpse into the reader's interactions with the text from which patterns emerge to inform instructional practice. Readers interact with text, thereby creating their own text, their own meaning (Rosenblatt 1978). As demonstrated throughout this book, readers miscue because they are attempting to construct meaning from text and sometimes this results in the creation of parallel texts, such as Steve's miscue of "the mayor smiling" for *and Mayor Smiley*. These constructions may or may not change the meaning of the text. In fact, occasionally, the reader's miscue may clarify the intended meaning with, say, the deletion of a word that clutters the text and interferes with the reader's ability to maintain meaning.

Teaching reading represents more than listening to children read and assisting them with word solving and comprehension. Reading must be directed toward empowering readers to use their miscues as interpretations of text that guide understanding and meaning. This process values and validates the reader's responses (Gilles and Dickinson 2000; Goodman and Marek 1996).

In the following chapter, we will discuss yet another dimension of RMA introduced in Chapter 4, called collaborative retrospective miscue analysis. The steps in the process are the same; however, the goal in CRMA is for the readers to independently discuss their miscues while the teacher observes, listens, and documents.

6

Gaining Independence
Collaborative Retrospective Miscue Analysis

I didn't know how to do that until Matt did that.
—Devon, a Seventh Grader

This chapter will

- define collaborative retrospective miscue analysis;
- examine the exploratory talk necessary for CRMA;
- explain the steps in CRMA; and
- explore the gradual release of responsibility from RMA to CRMA.

Defining Collaborative Retrospective Miscue Analysis

Collaborative retrospective miscue analysis originated with Sarah Costello, whose purpose was to "document what happens when students with a range of proficiencies work together in a small collaborative group and talk about reading miscues" (1996, 174). Sarah presented lessons to the whole class about miscues and reading strategies. She then had a group of four students engage in CRMA twice a week. The group met for a fifty-minute period, with the teacher present for about ten minutes. Each student read a text aloud and the group processed that text the following day. She observed the following about these seventh graders:

> The depth of the discussions and the interpretations that went on in these groups over eight weeks make it clear that when CRMA sessions are embedded into a classroom structure where discussion of the reading process is a part of the ongoing language arts curriculum, the proficiency of readers increases dramatically. (175)

Building on Costello's work, we have defined CRMA as a collaborative effort among students assigned to small groups to discuss miscues and retellings without the continuous or direct guidance of a teacher. CRMA may be conducted with proficient readers as well as those who struggle. When forming CRMA groups with struggling readers, we have found that placing students with somewhat similar reading abilities together provides more opportunities for growth. Placing a struggling reader in a group with highly proficient readers may embarrass the reader who has difficulty and hinder her more than help her. We know that CRMA works well with intermediate through high school readers; however, that should not discourage teachers from trying this strategy with younger readers as others have (see Appendix H).

Examining the Exploratory Talk Behind CRMA

One of the reasons that CRMA is so powerful is that through talk, students discover more about the reading process and themselves as readers. During CRMA students engage in *exploratory talk*, that hesitant, halting, rough-draft kind of talk in which students build on one another's comments to create new meanings and gain new insights (Barnes [1975] 1992; Pierce and Gilles 1993). Of course exploratory talk is important in RMA as well. Discoveries in the discussion, such as in Chapter 5 when Nathan miscued "caffeine" instead of *coffee*, are examples of exploratory talk. Remember that Justin replied, "I think he [Nathan] was kind of turning the word inside out to get it." Justin made a leap in his own thinking by considering Nathan's miscue. Justin realized that readers can sometimes manipulate words to gain meaning and Nathan was made more conscious of what he did as a reader. Together they each created new meaning; both readers were changed by that conversation.

In order for exploratory talk to occur, there must be trust in the group (Pierce and Gilles 1993). Students will not feel comfortable commenting on a miscue or be able to learn from one another if trust has not been built. Taking the time to form a solid classroom community is vital to the success of CRMA groups. If trust is lacking, the conversations may be brief and surface-level. Thus, many teachers do not attempt CRMA until after a strong classroom community has been built. Teachers begin to build trust in those first days of school when they engage students in getting-to-know-you activities. Building trust continues through literacy strategies like paired reading, literature study, and text coding discussions. Opportunities for pairs or small groups to read, talk, and think together build a trusting community.

As students in the CRMA group talk about a miscue and why the reader made it, a number of things happen in their thinking about reading. Many confirm the kinds of reading strategies they use. They realize that other students miscue for the same reasons that they do; perhaps the author was not clear, the text was misleading, or their background experience prompted them to alter the text. Also, as readers find that many other students make substitutions, they have renewed confidence in themselves to produce meaningful substitutions. The process of revaluing begins.

During CRMA, a student's thinking may be challenged by another in her group. Questions such as "Why did the reader miscue?" and "Why did you say that?" encourage students to examine their thought processes. These kinds of questions may have never been asked of them before. Many readers never consider why they miscued. They are convinced that all miscues are mistakes and they simply need to correct them. Suddenly, a peer is asking them questions about their thinking rather than correcting their decoding errors. This questioning process helps the students begin to be metacognitive and talk about their thinking. As they try to explain what they have done, they have to articulate their thinking, making their reading strategies and models of reading explicit for themselves and for others. Oftentimes, peers can help one another with this explicitness even more than teachers, because students accept challenges to their thinking more readily from their peers.

As students collaborate with one another, they are living proof of Vygotsky's zone of proximal development (1978). When students read challenging texts, they make miscues. Through the peer talk about those miscues, they begin to learn what kinds of miscues change the meaning and need correction and what kinds need not be corrected. They learn how to consistently monitor their reading for meaning.

Each CRMA conversation is largely dependent on the members in the group. Topics emerge naturally from their reading. After the CRMA conversations, readers use the information they have learned to be more independent in their reading. As Costello (1996) found, readers become more proficient after taking part in CRMA conversations.

The Process of CRMA

For students to conduct CRMA sessions independently, the teacher must set the stage carefully. Students need to learn what a miscue is, how miscues are marked and coded, and how to conduct the sessions. Many teachers use whole-group lessons to teach these concepts. Teachers may teach minilessons on such topics as what a miscue is, smart miscues, how we mark miscues, and how we can learn more about our reading through miscue analysis. Listening to an audiotaped recording of a student reading, viewing miscues from a recording sheet on the overhead projector, and exploring why the reader miscued are powerful demonstrations to students of how the talk in CRMA groups should proceed. Charts such as those Vicki posts (as described in Chapter 4) are also essential. These charts contain miscue markings and terms, such as *smart miscues, placeholders, sub-*

stitutions, omissions, insertions, retelling, and *repetitions,* as well as the reading strategies the students have been practicing. Having these terms visible helps students focus and be more independent. Vicki's students, who were moving from using RMA to using CRMA, initially consulted the charts frequently, but this lessened as sessions progressed and students gained confidence in the process.

Teachers conduct CRMA sessions using the following steps:

1. Prior to the CRMA session, students record themselves reading texts selected for miscue analysis by the teacher.
2. The teacher codes the miscues on the typescript and makes copies of the coded text for the students. (After practice with CRMA, students may be taught to code the miscues, which eliminates one step for the teacher.)
3. During the CRMA session, the students listen to the taped reading and stop the tape player when they want to discuss a miscue or some aspect of the retelling.

When first beginning CRMA groups, the teacher may suggest specific miscues for the group to consider for discussion. For example, the teacher may choose smart miscues to convince readers that not all miscues are equal. If students are overcorrecting, the teacher may choose miscues that students changed that still held the meaning. The conversation would then focus on why these miscues do not need to be corrected. Discussion during CRMA can focus on thinking about words, ideas, the plot, or interpretations. Discussing the various kinds of connections that students are making with the text is an excellent way to strengthen comprehension.

The teacher may or may not be present in CRMA conversations, but he does not direct the discussion; that is left to the students. Even so, when the teacher is present in groups, his input is important. As a more advanced reader, the teacher asks questions or makes comments that push students' thinking. He interprets inconsistencies in the conversation and intervenes when students are stuck on how to interpret reading behavior. The teacher can also tape-record the CRMA session to help plan for further instruction. Videotaping instead of audiotaping is also useful. The tape can be used as an informal assessment of readers or to generate topics for reading minilessons.

For struggling readers, especially, some initial experience in RMA with the teacher facilitating, choosing miscues for discussion, and participating in the conversation is strongly recommended before moving on to CRMA.

By focusing on Vicki, we can see an example of a fifth-grade teacher who transitioned from RMA to CRMA with her students. Vicki's students tape their own readings, she codes the miscues and gives them a copy, and the students select the miscues for discussion. Her students use the following questions to guide their conversations:

1. Does the miscue make sense?
2. Does it change the meaning of the sentence?
3. Why do you think the reader miscued?

Vicki often adds one additional question: What connections are you making to the text? This question helps readers keep the idea of making connections uppermost in their minds. CRMA is flexible in that oral miscues, the retellings, or both may guide the conversation. With high school readers, Chris (see Chapter 8) discovered that oral miscues may not be the most useful or interesting focus of the CRMA conversation; rather, the interpretation of the text, the number of details retold, and the degree of comprehension might be more significant. Her students did reiterate that oral reading was a necessary learning tool because it was important to read with intonation and fluency.

From RMA to CRMA: A Gradual Release of Responsibility

It is possible for CRMA students to be completely independent of the teacher, as demonstrated in the work of Costello (1992, 1996). Older students who have learned the miscue coding conduct miscue analysis without the teacher's help. They then choose the miscues for CRMA conversations (Costello 1992, 1996; Goodman and Flurkey 1996).

We consider RMA and CRMA to be on a continuum in terms of teacher input and student responsibility. Figure 6–1 demonstrates this continuum.

We envision the RMA–CRMA continuum as moving from teacher-directed to increasingly student-led conversations. At the beginning of RMA the teacher asks specific questions; however, as students and teachers become more comfortable with the procedure, the questions feel natural and are asked by the students and the teacher. When the teacher feels the students are able to conduct the groups on their own, she begins to withdraw. Vicki recalled, "I finally got smarter and learned to turn my chair away from the group, which led to their taking responsibility." Jennifer (in Chapter 7) told the boys she was working with that she would not talk as much in the groups anymore. Students need these overt signs that they are being asked to direct their groups.

We have found that with struggling readers there is also the potential for a gradual release of responsibility from RMA to CRMA. Pearson and Gallagher (1983) suggest that in many types of learning, the teacher begins by having the responsibility for the task and gradually turns over responsibility to the students.

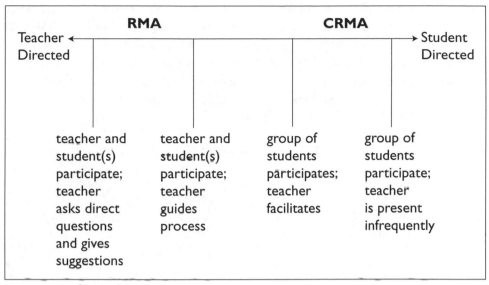

RMA		CRMA	
Teacher ← Directed			→ Student Directed
teacher and student(s) participate; teacher asks direct questions and gives suggestions	teacher and student(s) participate; teacher guides process	group of students participates; teacher facilitates	group of students participate; teacher is present infrequently

Figure 6–1. RMA–CRMA Continuum

We believe that moving from RMA to CRMA is similar to this process. In RMA, teachers conduct the miscue analysis, code the miscues, and select specific miscues for the conversation. They direct the conversation. In CRMA, the teachers may still select materials for students to read and provide the structure in the classroom to make these conversations work. They may choose, in the beginning, to be present for a large part of the conversation, and as students gain more independence, they may withdraw completely. In the first CRMA sessions they may ask some questions and then later move their chairs to the outside of the group, and finally relay full responsibility for the group meeting to its student members, letting the group meet on its own. Eventually students assume the responsibility for selecting the miscues and leading the conversations.

As the responsibility of the group is released from the teacher to the students, ownership increases. The students feel that the group belongs to them, not the teacher. As students learn about their own reading processes, and become stronger readers, they are empowered and revalued. Empowerment is the real benefit of RMA and CRMA. Success begets success; empowered readers want to read more.

Summing It Up and Moving On

This chapter defines collaborative miscue analysis and outlines the steps necessary for its implementation. The power of CRMA is in the talk among the readers;

therefore, establishing trust and respect among group members is imperative. For struggling readers we advocate a gradual release of responsibility from RMA to CRMA, since there are often issues of trust, confidence, and motivation that must first be addressed before CRMA can work. In Chapter 7, we describe Jennifer's work with two seventh-grade boys labeled learning disabled. Her story clearly illustrates the importance of building trust during RMA conversations with students. She found that RMA and CRMA helped these boys revalue themselves, and each other, as readers. In Chapter 8, Chris' CRMA work with high school students emphasizes how CRMA can be used as the foundation for curriculum planning.

7

Changing Attitudes, Changing Readers
Two Seventh Graders Move from RMA to CRMA

*We did something [with you] that we really didn't do before. We got
to pick whatever books we want, read and talk about it. Me and
Devon have probably got our reading a little better since we met you
probably. I think I have a lot.*

—Matt, a Seventh Grader

This chapter will

- demonstrate the power of RMA as part of the revaluing process;
- explain the role of talk in the RMA process; and
- explore how CRMA works with preadolescents labeled learning disabled.

Beginning the RMA Journey

The above comment from Matt occurred near the end of the time that Jennifer worked with Devon and Matt, two seventh-grade students labeled learning disabled who spent their days in a special education classroom. Jennifer's goal was to help struggling readers become more proficient. She did this by beginning with RMA and eventually moving to CRMA. And Matt was right—neither of the boys had ever done anything like this before!

Devon and Matt spent most of their academic lives in special education classrooms. They had failed often and been told many times by others that they were not smart. As a result, they created behaviors to avert teachers, thus avoiding situations in which they would be unsuccessful. With this RMA–CRMA project, Devon and Matt were once again being asked to work on reading, which was extremely difficult for them and would leave them vulnerable. The first barrier Jennifer had to overcome was their personal opinions about reading and of themselves as readers.

Devon and Matt worked with Jennifer regularly during the school year. To begin, she conducted a Burke Reading Interview, and then she saw each of them twice for an individual miscue analysis and an RMA conversation with her. Next, Jennifer worked with the boys for three RMA sessions, three CRMA sessions, and one post-interview. In the midst of the CRMA sessions, Jennifer realized Devon needed to revalue himself as a reader. She was able to hold two additional RMA sessions with Devon because Matt was absent. This additional time provided opportunities to work with Devon individually and help him find ways of valuing himself as a reader.

The Burke Reading Interview

Before asking the boys to read with her, Jennifer administered the Burke Reading Interview (Goodman, Watson, and Burke 1987). As described earlier, the Burke Interview reveals a reader's perceptions of reading and the reading process. As Jennifer talked with Matt about his reading, she learned that he relied heavily on a single strategy: sounding out. When asked how he would help someone having trouble as a reader, he suggested, "Try to find a word that's in the word that they know and then try to sound it out." Matt used this sound-it-out strategy consistently, but ineffectively, during his reading.

As Jennifer walked with Devon to a quiet place to conduct his Burke Reading Interview, he asked, "Will you help me to read?" This indicated that Devon wanted to learn to read, even though he believed he was a poor reader. He said he had three strategies: skip it, sound it out, and ask a teacher. Jennifer saw all three of those strategies in use when Devon was reading. In the Burke Reading Interview, Devon revealed that he had younger brothers and sisters with whom he read. He told this story about his brother, although he could have as easily told it about himself: "He memorizes the book and then every day he'll come home and sometimes he'll get something wrong and then he'll look at the pictures. Then like two days later you ask him to read the book again and he don't know it." Devon, too, looked at pictures when he was stuck during his reading. He, too, talked about memorizing words. Devon told Jennifer several parables about people he knew or characters on television who had trouble with reading. These parables always resembled Devon's situation and revealed to Jennifer how Devon viewed himself as a reader.

Conducting Individual Miscue and RMA Sessions

Because neither Devon nor Matt had participated in anything like miscue analysis or RMA before, Jennifer met with each for an individual miscue analysis and RMA session. Jennifer wanted them to feel confident and comfortable with the process before she placed them together for RMA. The first individual session was with Matt.

Matt

The reading teacher had stated previously that the boys were interested in World War II, so Jennifer selected three books about World War II from which they could choose to read. Matt chose *The Hindenburg* (O'Brien 2000) for his miscue session. *The Hindenburg* is about the first dirigibles that flew during World War II and is appropriate for students in fifth or sixth grade, although it has some difficult vocabulary. Matt said he chose *The Hindenburg* because it "looked cool" and "it blows up." As Matt read aloud he struggled with words and read haltingly. He diligently read to the end even though he made numerous miscues. After he read the book, Jennifer asked Matt to retell what he remembered. Because he seemed hesitant, Jennifer suggested he draw a picture to help him remember. As he drew a picture of the dirigible, Matt retold the basic plot of the story and could recall some of the details when prompted. Though his retelling was brief, it had surprisingly more details than one would expect after listening to him struggle with the reading. This underscored the importance of the retelling and allowed Jennifer to gain a more holistic look at Matt beyond his oral fluency. From listening to the taped retelling, Jennifer learned that Matt understood the story at a basic level even though he had miscued frequently.

After the miscue session, Jennifer analyzed Matt's reading. She found that he relied heavily on graphophonic cueing. In other words, he sounded out unfamiliar words, often substituting the word in the text with a nonword rather than a word that might fit semantically in the sentence. For example:

$eggsurious

0203   modern, the most luxurious, the fastest, the largest.

In this example, Matt substituted a nonword, "eggsurious," for the word *luxurious*. Though he tried that word only once, several of Matt's miscues included as many as four or five unsuccessful attempts before moving on to the next word. For example:

UC stucks UC
sticks emergency
state exeme–
sta– e–

2902   Eckner felt that there was static electricity in the air because of

Here, Matt struggled over two words: *static* and *electricity*. He attempted both words first with a partial word ("sta-" and "exeme-") and then began to try words

73

that had high graphophonemic similarities (e.g., "state" and "sticks"). Matt's miscues suggest he began by sounding out a word by letter, then moved to sampling initial and ending letters. Though Matt did not leave a nonword in this example, the words he left are not semantically similar, suggesting that he may not have been reading for meaning.

Though Matt relied heavily on the sounding-out strategy, he also repeated and self-corrected occasionally. These strategies demonstrated that Matt was self-monitoring at times and suggested that he may have been reading for meaning in certain parts of the text. He also revised sentences into his own words and often inserted words to make a sentence read more smoothly. Though these strategies appeared in the miscue analysis, they seemed to be strategies that Matt was either unaware that he was using or unable to articulate during the Burke Reading Interview.

Jennifer began Matt's RMA session by pointing out his high-level miscues. Encouraging the boys to see miscues as a normal part of the reading process was important during the individual sessions. Jennifer encouraged them to view miscues as a vehicle for understanding their own reading strategies. The first miscue Matt and Jennifer examined was on line 1201:

1201   In 1939, the *Graf Zeppelin* began to make regular trips carrying
                                                                      (c) care-fully

          paying

Matt read "carefully" for *carrying* and then self-corrected it. When Jennifer asked him what he was thinking, he responded, "I thought that they were carrying them carefully, but *carefully* doesn't have two *r*s." He recognized that his first attempt did not fit with the clues from the text, which led him to correct this miscue. In reviewing this miscue with Matt, Jennifer initiated a discussion about predicting and how good readers often make predictions, then change them if the text clues do not fit their predicted meaning.

Matt was quiet and somewhat dismissive throughout the first session. He answered many of Jennifer's questions with "I don't know," "I don't remember anything," and "I can't remember what I was thinking." He did not elaborate when prompted and often answered in one-word responses. However, as the RMA conversation continued, Matt began to show more interest in what was happening. This is common behavior for adolescents in special education classes. In the past Matt found that teachers often left him alone if he gave short, dismissive answers, thus removing himself from the difficult tasks. Eventually, Matt became interested as Jennifer consistently pointed out the effective things he did as a reader. She continued to not only boost his view of himself as a reader but also reinforce the useful strategies he employed.

Jennifer continued the RMA by showing Matt examples of reading strategies she saw him use. Once he became engaged in the process, she invited Matt to listen to the tape and stop it when he heard a miscue he wanted to talk about. He stopped the tape on lines 205 and 206. Here Matt struggled on two words: *Hindenburg* and *unforgettable*.

205   it. For passengers who flew on the *Hindenburg,* the experience was

206   unforgettable.

Matt struggled with *Hindenberg*, then substituted a nonword, "unforgottable," for *unforgettable*. Matt and Jennifer's conversation follows:

MATT: I still can't get it right (*referring to* Hindenberg).

TEACHER: What did you do here?

MATT: I tried to say it a whole bunch of different ways.

TEACHER: What were you trying for?

MATT: Say it right?

TEACHER: And you didn't get it, did you? So what did you do?

MATT: I went on.

TEACHER: You went on. Right, and that was probably a good thing to do. Let's keep reading that sentence. "The experience was . . . "

MATT: Unforgettable.

TEACHER: It is *unforgettable* and you said "unforgottable." What do you think? What did you do there?

MATT: They're both the same, sort of.

TEACHER: They are both the same? Same meaning? Is there a meaning change?

MATT: Sort of, because they are two different words, but saying the same thing.

Matt not only realized his miscue ("unforgottable" for *unforgettable*) but was able to articulate what he did as a reader ("went on") and his analysis of the miscue ("they are two different words, but saying the same thing"). It is important to note here that Jennifer chose not to further discuss the *Hindenburg* miscue for two reasons: First, it was a proper noun. Jennifer knew that proper nouns can be pronounced in a myriad of ways, so focusing on the pronunciation of the name would be counterproductive. Also, Matt was relying heavily on sounding out and she wanted to extend him to other strategies. At this point Jennifer did not feel Matt was confident enough to be pushed outside his comfort zone to take a greater risk with his reading.

Jennifer's goal in Matt's RMA session was to help him revalue himself as a reader by showing him the effective strategies he used (Goodman and Marek 1996). At the end of the RMA session, Matt picked up the typescript that was lying on the table between them. He looked over the entire typescript. "I do all these things good?" he asked. Jennifer nodded and Matt continued, "Do you think I could have a copy of this to give to my mom? I didn't know I was that kind of reader. You know, a good reader." Matt's statement about himself affirmed to Jennifer that he had begun the process of revaluing himself as a reader. Ken Goodman (1996b) believes that revaluing helps readers "come to appreciate their own strengths, to recognize the productive strategies they already use, and to build positively on those" (17).

Devon

The book that Devon read for Jennifer during the individual miscue analysis session, *Zipping, Zapping, Zooming Bats* (Earle 1997), was a nonfiction picture book about bats, appropriate for students in second or third grade. As Jennifer listened to Devon read, she noticed immediately that he skipped not only several words per page but also several pages in the book. On most pages, Devon skipped anywhere from four to ten words. He often paused before he skipped the words, though this was not always the case. His reading was hesitant and his frustration showed immediately. Devon said he liked to watch shows like *Discovery* and *Animal Kingdom* on television, so he knew a lot about bats before reading the book. This might explain why his retelling was strong, though much of it was guided.

In analyzing the recording of Devon's reading, Jennifer confirmed that he relied heavily on one strategy: skipping unknown words. If he didn't know a word, he would skip it and never return to it. Observing this behavior, Jennifer knew Devon didn't trust himself much as a reader. Devon's strengths were his few high-level miscues, including self-correcting, repeating for meaning, and substituting semantically acceptable words or phrases.

Jennifer's first goal for Devon, as for Matt, was to help him revalue himself as a reader. Devon, however, was not an easy sell. When Jennifer pointed out a high-level miscue to him, he was skeptical of the concept that all readers miscue and some miscues are a sign of good reading. For example, on line 2501, Devon substituted the word "to" for the word *into*.

2501   If you go in̶t̶o̶ a cave in June or July, be sure to look for baby

*(handwritten above "into": **to**)*

The following conversation represents Devon's understanding:

DEVON: I put "to" and skipped out the *in*. It is supposed to read "If you go into a cave in June or July."
TEACHER: Why do you think you did that?
DEVON: I didn't see it.
TEACHER: Does it make sense if I say, "If you go to a cave in June or July" ?
DEVON: Yeah.
TEACHER: Yeah. So did you need to correct it?
DEVON: (*Nods*)
TEACHER: You think you should have?
DEVON: No. I didn't have to.
TEACHER: You didn't have to? Why?
DEVON: Because it made sense.

It was only after Jennifer's prompting that Devon conceded that he did not need to correct the miscue.

Devon had also learned to develop "protective strategies" throughout his school life (Blumenfeld and Marx 1997, 81) such as giving answers like "I don't know" to avoid trusting someone else's response to him. His lack of trust in Jennifer was evident. When Jennifer invited Devon to choose the miscues he wanted to talk about, he said, "I don't know." And many times throughout the RMA when Jennifer asked Devon about what he was thinking, he answered, "Nothing. I don't think."

It was clear after working with the boys individually that bringing them together might be a challenge. It would take time for Jennifer to gain their trust and for them to trust each another.

RMA Sessions

Both boys had different strengths coming into the RMA sessions and neither had ever talked about the reading process, much less his own metacognitive reading process. Jennifer explained they were going to do a slightly shorter version of what they had done during her past visits. Jennifer chose to follow a process similar to that used by Chris Worsnop and Debra Jacobson (Goodman and Marek 1996), who had students listen to one another read with "miscue ears" and then talk about those miscues. Jennifer brought in three to four nonfiction texts to use during the RMA visit with the intention of having each boy choose a short excerpt to read while the other would circle the miscues he heard during the reading. Jennifer intended to tape-record the reading and have the boys listen to the tape. However, the boys did not like to hear themselves read on the tape. In fact, they were worried Jennifer would "juice them" (share the tapes of their reading with other teachers in the building). So instead, they listened to each other read a whole excerpt of text, marked the miscues, and then discussed them. Jennifer did, however, tape their conversations so she could analyze them. Jennifer's role was to guide and mediate the conversation that followed the reading, making sure the boys' feedback remained positive and constructive. Since the boys read on different levels with varying strengths and strategies (i.e., Matt relied heavily on sounding it out and Devon relied heavily on skipping), Jennifer was uncertain of what to expect from the RMA. What she found was something like climbing a mountain: a long hike up but a beautiful view at the top.

The first three sessions with the boys were difficult. They spent much of their time participating in the disruptive behaviors they used in their self-contained classroom. Such "protective strategies" (Blumenfeld and Marx 1997, 81) could be seen in much of the talk that occurred during these first few sessions. These behaviors were their way of protecting themselves from having to read, thereby making themselves less vulnerable to criticism from Jennifer or from each other. For example, one of Devon's first comments about Matt's miscue markings was "He don't even know what he put." The boys used this type of talk to redirect attention and, in so doing, took the focus off themselves.

They also tried to sabotage the sessions. Though it was exasperating at the time, Jennifer realized the boys were looking for ways to "save face" and maintain their "cool" demeanor. Struggling learners, especially adolescents labeled learning disabled, often try to sabotage the instructional process when they are beginning to do well because, in their view, it is impossible to succeed. They believe it is better to undermine the progress than accept a different view of themselves. Students who have experienced many years of failure begin to define themselves by that failure; therefore, when they are faced with success, they often retreat.

Their sabotaging behaviors included acting confused about page numbers or where they were in the text. Although many times this was used to clarify things for themselves, they also used this confusion as a way to change the subject or redirect attention. It was a defense mechanism much like learned helplessness

(Covington 1983). They would say things like "Where do I start?"; "Where's he at?"; "Where's it at?"; "What you talking about?"; and "What word is it?"

As the sessions progressed the boys took small positive steps. Devon and Matt began putting themselves into the other's thought processes. They began to hypothesize why the other made a miscue. For example, Devon, in talking about one of Matt's miscues, said:

> He mispronounced it. And on this one he skipped it. 'Cause I think he didn't see it; then he went back to it. This one he didn't pronounce it right, no he skipped it then came back. He tried to pronounce it, but he didn't get it.

The boys also collaborated to figure out words. In fact, word-solving collaboration was their first engagement in RMA and appeared consistently throughout the sessions. Jennifer believed they adopted this type of collaboration initially because it felt safer to work together than to take the risk alone. Following is an example of this type of collaboration. In the example, Devon was discussing Matt's miscue on the word *laterally* (in reference to a type of pass in the game of polo).

MATT: It's throwing it to a teammate.
TEACHER: It says, "To hit the ball forward or _____ to a teammate." So I am either going to hit it . . .
DEVON: A pass.
TEACHER: It is kind of like a pass, and a pass can be forward or a pass can be what?
MATT: Sideways.
DEVON: Diagonal.
TEACHER: Sideways or diagonal . . .
MATT: Behind.
DEVON: Lateral!

In this example, the boys worked together to figure the word out with Jennifer's guidance. Eventually, Devon found the word that worked best. Here, they were focusing on meaning. Other times they focused more on sounding out or substituting a synonym. When the synonym strategy did not work for them, they would again resort to graphophonic cues. This excerpt also shows the extent to which Jennifer was involved in the initial conversations.

After the first few sessions, Devon and Matt began to talk about reading strategies using miscue terminology. Matt learned about high- and low-level miscues, describing high-level miscues as "doing something good like correcting and making meaning." Devon talked about "going back and correcting stuff in your head" and "using different words that mean the same word." During one of these exchanges when they were talking about strategies, Jennifer asked them if they were doing anything different when they read since they started their "talks" about reading. Matt said, "We do better stuff when we read."

Devon said, "I know I can do it [read]. I just don't like to."

During their RMA conversations, Devon and Matt provided Jennifer with insight into how they saw themselves as learners. The boys lamented the fact that they were in the special education classroom. Matt said, "We hate the retarded class." And later, in another RMA session, they talked more about their attitudes toward themselves as readers. Devon claimed he was a "bad" reader "because if I knew how to read, I wouldn't be here."

Matt, who had a slightly better image of himself as a reader, responded to Devon, saying, "It's all about our behavior; that's why we're in that [special education] class."

In the third session, the boys began to accept more responsibility. Devon asked Matt about a miscue Devon had made: "Did I go back and correct this or did I skip it?" It was the first time Devon showed an interest in the strategy he had used. He let his guard down and felt comfortable asking Matt about his reading behavior. Matt accepted responsibility as well when he said, "I said that one, but I didn't get it right completely." This was a breakthrough for the boys. It was one of the first times they dropped the pretense of not caring about reading and not thinking of themselves as readers.

Reflecting on the Process

At the end of the first semester, Jennifer stepped back to reflect on the RMA group. She was encouraged that the boys were dropping the protective strategies, yet she felt as if the sessions were not progressing as well as expected. She realized that some of this was due to her own teaching behaviors, so she changed three aspects of her instruction.

First, Jennifer changed the focus of the RMA to CRMA. She decided to look at the transcripts through student talk. Also, she chose to change the structure of the discussions. Mehan (1979) suggests that teachers' classroom talk often follows a structure of teacher stimulus, student response, and teacher evaluation. RMA sessions with Devon and Matt thus far seemed to follow Mehan's structure: Jennifer asked a question, the boys answered, and then Jennifer evaluated their answer. She decided to release the responsibility of learning to the boys and, initially, pull back from the conversations almost completely. When Jennifer met with Devon and Matt during the second semester she told them she would not talk as much as she had in previous sessions.

The second and most helpful modification Jennifer made to the process was working with Devon one-on-one before bringing the boys together again. Because

Devon struggled more than Matt, he compared himself with Matt and his attitude was negative. In Jennifer's RMA session with him, she walked him through his transcript, focusing on his high-level miscues and showing him all the good strategies he was using as a reader. Though this was teacher directed at first, as Devon began to believe in his strengths, he joined the conversation, thus providing Jennifer with new insights into his metacognitive process.

The third modification was unplanned. In the past the boys and Jennifer had sat in a horseshoe with her on one end and the boys next to each other on the other end of the horseshoe. By accident one day, Jennifer sat between the boys. It made all the difference. They were now looking at each other while talking, which made their communication more immediate and stronger.

CRMA Sessions

With the new changes, Jennifer and the boys began CRMA in the second semester. It was awkward at first for Devon and Matt to do most of the talking, but they soon became engaged as they realized Jennifer was giving them the responsibility and ownership of the CRMA conversation.

As the boys took the lead during these sessions, they unknowingly changed the format. Instead of reading a whole excerpt and then discussing it, they began to read a paragraph at a time, talking about the miscues within each paragraph before moving on. Sometimes they even talked about a miscue at the sentence level. Their modification enabled them to remember the miscues and practice their thinking in shorter chunks. This process worked well for the boys. It provided more immediate feedback and allowed them to check their comprehension more frequently.

Word Work

The boys began to collaborate to figure out words. In the following excerpt, Devon miscued on the word *centuries*:

MATT: Countries.
DEVON: Countries? That's not countries.
TEACHER: How do you know?
DEVON: It's *tur* in the middle of it and *ies* at the end of it.
MATT: Centuries.
DEVON: Centuries *(he continues to read)* ago . . .

In this example, Matt suggested a word but Devon provided a reason that the word did not match the text. Jennifer's role in this example was to encourage the boys to explicate their reasoning, although she did not evaluate the response. The boys worked together to help each other with unfamiliar text.

New Strategies

As the boys collaborated to figure out words, they unconsciously shared strategies with each other. In the previous example, Devon shared with Matt the strategy of breaking down the word. In that same example, Matt shared with Devon his strategy of "guessing words that might fit the sentence." Sharing strategies carried over into other CRMA conversations as the boys began to experiment with different strategies. For example, Matt tried Devon's strategy of using a placeholder when he said, "The blank. I am just gonna say that." Devon suggested to Matt a new strategy he learned during CRMA when he said, "Skip it and *come back to it.*" Recall that Devon earlier skipped text but never returned to it. The boys' articulation of these strategies demonstrated not only that they were taking risks within their reading but that they also were confident in sharing new strategies with another reader. They had begun to use CRMA effectively.

Engagement and Strategy Use

As the boys shared strategies with each other, they used them more often. They naturally became more engaged in the texts as they began to feel more confident and prepared to handle unfamiliar words or phrases. They became more empowered as readers and thinkers. As their confidence grew, the boys felt more comfortable being metacognitive about their reading strategies. Davenport (1993) refers to metacognition as "thinking about your own thinking" (188). Matt said of his miscue on the word *habitat*, "I was just thinking about different *h* words that would fit there. Then I said them all and one of them seemed to sound like it would fit." Devon, too, showed signs of metacognition when he spoke about his miscue on the word *rangers*. He said, "I was like, I said they did not put out the fire. I knew that it had to have someone put out the fire and it [the word] was rangers."

Confidence and engagement were also reflected in the boys' reading behavior. For example, the next excerpt shows Devon struggling on a word:

DEVON: In-, enco-, encouraging! En- . . . I know it is *in* and *could*, right? In . . . could . . .

MATT: That's right.

DEVON: *Into* . . . I'm trying.

MATT: OK, I'll give you this . . .

DEVON: Hold up, I got it: soldiers from the U.S. Army, *even? Including!* Soldiers.

In this excerpt, Devon said, "Hold up," to slow down Matt's help. This gave him time to think and work on the word. It let Jennifer know that he was truly engaged in the text as well as in the process of reading.

The boys also began to use their new strategies in other reading. For example, the following excerpt shows the boys using their background knowledge to understand the word *planetarium*:

DEVON: I was like, then I read it and I knew 'cause I watch *Jurassic Park 2*, that's what helped me out 'cause, like, whenever they were like this is a bird cage. And like, it had to be like something they could fly around in. And somehow like to have stars and then I knew it.

TEACHER: Did you know that, Matt?

MATT: Uh-hm.

TEACHER: From the same thing, or how did you know it?

MATT: 'Cause how we went to there. And . . .

DEVON: Yeah and we saw the stars.

TEACHER: Really?

DEVON: Rockbridge.

MATT: I like going there. That was fun.

Here Devon and Matt activated prior knowledge to gain meaning from the text even though they relied on different memories. Devon drew from a movie he saw and Matt pulled from a field trip to the local high school planetarium.

Other strategies the boys used included looking at the pictures and connecting the text to something they knew. In the following excerpt the boys use picture clues to help with the word *hummingbirds*. Matt had just read a paragraph about hummingbirds.

TEACHER: How did you know it was *hummingbirds*?

DEVON: He looked at the picture.

MATT: I looked at the picture.

TEACHER: In the picture?

DEVON: You can see the long beak.

TEACHER: I didn't know that from that picture. That's really good.

DEVON: And then, like, and then, like, he looked at the word and then he knew.

Here both boys used picture clues to help them work out the word. Though Jennifer was unfamiliar with the characteristics that distinguished a hummingbird from other types of birds, both boys knew that information. This was a time when the collaborative aspect truly benefited them: the strategy of using picture clues was validated by a peer. This made a much stronger impact than would the teacher suggesting they use a particular strategy. Notice that even though Jennifer was still involved, her role changed from directing the conversation to being more of a member in the conversation.

CRMA *Grows*

Once the boys had become readers who used a variety of strategies, who were engaged in the text, and who felt confident as learners, they began to be truly collaborative. They confidently suggested specific strategies for the other to use while reading. They became excited about reading, often working together to challenge and support each other. In the following example, Matt paused for a moment to figure out the word *blanket* and said "blanketed." When he finished the section, Jennifer asked to talk about that miscue.

TEACHER: Let's talk about that.
DEVON: How did you get that one, Matt?
MATT: Uh, I saw *blank* and . . .
DEVON: *-ket* like in *ball, basketball*, right?
MATT: Then I was like, *blanket*, and then I was going to read it as *blanket* and then I read "blanketed." (*He continues to read.*)

In this conversation, Devon took charge and asked Matt to explain how he was able to figure out the word. Ultimately, the boys collaborated to explain how Matt used the strategy of finding a word within a word.

As Matt and Devon became more successful, their enthusiasm for reading increased. In the next example, the boys had been reading about animals:

DEVON: Can we finish this book tomorrow?
TEACHER: Do you mean next week when I come?
DEVON: No, tomorrow.
TEACHER: I'm not coming tomorrow.
DEVON: You should come, like, every Thursday from now on.

Instead of being fearful of reading, Devon and Matt actually looked forward to their sessions with Jennifer. Their attitudes about reading and themselves as readers were changing.

Overall Devon and Matt showed a large range of emotions and behaviors during CRMA sessions. When Jennifer spoke with them in a postproject interview, they were not only able to articulate the process of CRMA but also told her about the knowledge they gained from each other. In the following excerpt, she asks the boys to identify what they did as readers as a result of their collaborative conversations:

TEACHER: Real quick, talk about some of the things that you did as a reader.

DEVON: Skipped it, sounded out, and then I, like, thought about what would go in its place.

MATT: I was thinking about the words that sort of sound like it and then I start to list them.

TEACHER: You really like the sound-out strategy, don't you? That works best for you?

DEVON: No, he likes trying to find out other words that would work.

MATT: I just do that.

DEVON: I didn't know how to do that until Matt did that.

Insights into RMA and CRMA

Jennifer's journey with the boys made clear to us the value RMA and CRMA hold for struggling adolescent readers like Matt and Devon and the students featured in the next chapter. How readers see themselves as learners and readers is instrumental to their success. Adolescents labeled learning disabled often have a strong history of failure. Like Matt and Devon, they believe they *can't* read. They believe the ability to read is innate. Reading is something they cannot do, even if they work and try hard. Jennifer found Matt's and Devon's initial behaviors were a strong match with the characteristics of students who have an entity theory of learning (Dweck and Bempechet 1983): they gave up quickly when reading; they struggled to stay focused; they did not use metacognitive strategies; and they did not learn from their miscues (Kaplan and Maehr 1997; Henson and Gilles 2003). They took fewer risks "to avoid judgments of incompetence" (Dweck and Bempechet 1983, 250). This was obvious in the boys' first RMA sessions when they reverted to protective answers like "I don't know" or avoided the reading, rather than attempting an answer that might be wrong. Like other learners who hold an entity theory of learning, Matt and Devon perceived reading as skills driven; they believed good reading entailed perfect pronunciation of every word. Flawless reading was more important than comprehension, and comprehension meant getting the right answer (Blumenfeld and Marx 1997).

Through the conversations associated with RMA and CRMA, Jennifer helped Devon and Matt change their beliefs and reading behaviors. She provided opportunities to see that reading miscues were not errors; instead, they function as windows into the reader's thoughts. Devon and Matt learned that everyone, not just them, made miscues. CRMA helped Devon and Matt take control of their learning. In the first semester, Jennifer was more teacher directed in her approach to RMA. She modeled the kinds of questions she wanted the readers to ask about the miscues, such as "What did you say there?"; "Why did you do that?"; and "What were you thinking here?" She guided their conversations and showed them example upon example of their using solid strategies in their reading. Jennifer moved away from the extrinsic motivation to which they were accustomed, such as candy and stickers, and demonstrated the internal motivation that came from successful problem solving in their reading.

In the second semester Jennifer began CRMA and slowly released the control of the sessions to Matt and Devon. They chose books to read from three that she brought, deciding on the length of the text read, and the amount of time they spent talking about their miscues and retellings. The shorter amounts of reading enabled the boys to discuss miscues while the miscues were still fresh in their minds. This gradual release of responsibility also helped change the boys' theory of learning. Reading was not out of their grasp; they gained control of it.

Perhaps the most important element needed for the boys to change their views about themselves as readers was their relationship with Jennifer. They needed to see that she wanted them to learn and that she believed they could learn before they were willing to give the RMA process a chance. This was as important as the process itself. Had the boys not trusted Jennifer, they would have rejected RMA and remained true to the entity theory of learning. They might have gone through the motions of RMA without internalizing the process or benefiting from the results. Instead, after a great deal of work on building trust and understanding, the boys participated in authentic conversations about the reading strategies they used. They worked together and learned from each other. As Devon said toward the end of the year, "It's the best thing to do."

Summing It Up and Moving On

In this chapter RMA and CRMA were used with two seventh-grade boys labeled learning disabled. RMA and CRMA enabled the boys to use exploratory talk (Barnes 1996) as a tool for learning and gave them time to talk about their reading so they would learn and practice new reading strategies. More importantly, the sessions helped them revalue themselves as readers. As they learned to see themselves as learners and readers, they engaged in the process, took more risks, and were more successful and empowered. Through RMA and CRMA, these two adolescent boys grew as readers and learners. Chapter 8 introduces the use of CRMA in a high school language arts curriculum.

8

Constructing Personal and Social Literacies Through Text
RMA and CRMA in High School

What you read affects how you read.
—Brad, a High School Senior

This chapter will

- explore RMA and CRMA in an alternative high school setting;
- demonstrate the adaptability of RMA and CRMA for high school reading instruction;
- examine personal, social, and text connections through reading conferences, question-and-response, and CRMA; and
- demonstrate the importance of involving older learners in customizing and maintaining the RMA and CRMA processes.

Introducing RMA and CRMA into a High School Classroom

The opening quote is from a conversation between Brad and Chris, a high school language arts and reading specialist. At first Chris interpreted this remark superficially, thinking Brad was referring to pieces that were interesting or well written. However, after listening to responses and remarks during the various CRMA conversations as well as during individual RMA reading conferences with Brad, she realized Brad meant that the personal or social connections the reader makes to text defines his or her perceptions of what is being read, and ultimately how one reads or interprets the text.

Chris has been studying the use of RMA with readers between the ages of fourteen and twenty-three for more than eight years. Her students are males enrolled in language arts and reading classes in an alternative high school where Chris has taught for fourteen years (Moore and Aspegren 2000, 2001). Most of these males are identified as learning disabled, behavior disordered, or both. About 50 percent of her students are African American, 30 percent are Hispanic, and 20 percent are Caucasian. They come from a broad range of socioeconomic and family backgrounds, but according to Chris, they share one common characteristic: they need to better understand themselves as learners in order to more appropriately construct a personal and social identity. The entity theory of learning (Dweck and Bempechet 1983) is quite common in Chris' classroom. In other words, most of her students believe that the ability to learn is innate, perhaps because they have known nothing but failure in their lives. Others, however, realize working with Chris may be their last opportunity to do well enough in school to acquire a general equivalency diploma (GED). For many, it is their last chance to stay out of prison. Their attitudes toward learning are sometimes positively affected by their desire for social and personal survival. Key to supporting these attitudes is linking learning to social and personal interests, experiences, and literacies.

Chris' Interest and Beliefs in RMA

Since 1995, Chris has been working to learn how strategies and processes in RMA can assist adolescents who, regardless of reading fluency, consistently struggle with oral and silent reading comprehension and poor self-images of themselves as learners.

During her first RMA classroom inquiry, Chris focused on the analysis of oral miscues and retellings with a single case study, a student named Dan (Moore and Aspegren 2001). Dan struggled with both decoding and comprehension. During RMA conversations, Chris helped Dan view miscues as a means for understanding his own reading process rather than as signals of reading failure. At first, Dan relied heavily on graphophonic cues, but Chris guided him toward the use of context and meaning as more reliable reading strategies. Talking about reading miscues and giving retellings were new learning experiences for Dan, who seemed to benefit the most from having the time to talk about his reading with a knowledgeable conversation partner. Six months later, Dan showed strong gains in fluency and comprehension, and he was well on his way to completing the requirements for a general equivalency diploma (Moore and Aspegren 2001). On the school's criterion-referenced achievement test in reading administered prior to RMA sessions, Dan placed in the 26th percentile. Upon completion of his work with Chris, posttest reading scores placed him in the 44th percentile. Chris elaborated: "The students in my class are not there because they lack intelligence; they are there because they have misplaced values and goals" (Moore and Aspegren 2001, 493–94). Dan once explained his reading disability during an RMA session: "I know about a lot, but sometimes can't read the words that go with it" (Moore and Aspegren 2001, 492).

In her second classroom inquiry, Chris examined the use of RMA as a reading assessment and learning strategy with three older adolescent students from her class. These students volunteered to try this new strategy because they said they wanted to be better readers. Two of the three volunteers were reasonably fluent readers, but the retellings during their RMA conversations with Chris revealed they all lacked comprehension strategies that would allow them to think about text through their own experiences and knowledge. As work with these students progressed, Chris moved away from discussing oral miscues with the two more fluent readers and focused on emphasizing the retelling of strategic details to develop comprehension. Chris noticed that with each retelling, these two students became more engaged in the reading when they made personal, social, or life connections to the stories and/or connected previously read texts to what they were currently reading. As a result of her work, Chris realized the need for teachers to be flexible in their use of RMA. Certain aspects of the process might be more useful to classroom assessment and instruction than others, depending on factors of age, interests, fluency, and the comprehension strengths of the reader.

Customizing the RMA and CRMA Process

In her latest classroom inquiry, Chris took a different direction with RMA and CRMA to demonstrate how these methods can positively affect the social and personal literacies of struggling adolescents in an alternative high school setting. Based on her previous classroom research, Chris developed an implementation plan that she believed had potential for transforming her whole-class approach to high school reading instruction. Chris introduced audiotaped readings, retellings, individual conferencing, and rereading through RMA and extended those conversations to CRMA, using both as a framework for classroom reading instruction. Chris' students were not making meaningful connections to text that would allow them to interpret and discuss their reading beyond the surface level. The process of CRMA is concerned with providing students the support they need to make sense of what they read and to move toward deeper interpretations of text.

To assist these struggling adolescents to better understand themselves as readers and learners, Chris customized classroom reading instruction with the intention of helping the students make clearer connections to the reading process, themselves, other texts, and the world at large. The importance of questioning and talking about a text while making connections to other texts, to self, and to the world is well documented (Keene and Zimmermann 1997; Tovani 2000), but it is not necessarily well implemented by high school teachers (Tovani 2000). This was a bold new direction for Chris, who in the past had worked with only small RMA groups outside of regular class time, with a traditional focus on the analysis of oral miscues and retellings, while maintaining structured whole-class instruction.

Chris' Classroom

At the beginning of the new semester, there were eleven students in Chris' all-male class. Chris' classroom typically has between eleven and fifteen students who range between the ages of sixteen and twenty-one, but student attendance continually fluctuates—a nine-month placement is unusual. Her language arts and reading program must maintain consistency in assessment and instruction to allow students to move in and out of the system with some degree of documented accomplishment. Chris was not happy with the way the current program underserved student growth in academic, personal, and social literacy. She had not yet tried RMA with any of her students; to her knowledge, they had no background in examining miscues or retellings. She had observed that their assigned group literature discussions produced flat and literal understandings, signifying to Chris that their metacognitive skills, or ability to think about their own thinking, were underdeveloped (Davenport 2002).

What Wasn't Working?

Reading instruction in Chris' class followed this pattern prior to implementing classroom RMA and CRMA: students read silently, answered questions Chris had previously prepared, then discussed their answers in small groups. With this class in particular, Chris was concerned with the lack of substantive interaction that the after-reading discussions produced. She explained:

> I was hoping to encourage the students to have more of a sense that they knew what they just read and the connections between the questions and the text. When I asked how they did on the comprehension questions, their answers were glib. Some said, "I did good," or "I didn't do so great." I felt they should be making stronger connections to the readings and to the reading process itself, or even to the questions. They should have been better able to talk about the answers as well as the text. They felt they either knew the answer or they did not. It was as though there was something missing in their ability to interpret text through their own lives and experiences.

Creating Student Buy-In

Chris told the members of her language arts and reading class of her plans to change the established routine for reading instruction and asked for their voluntary participation. She explained to the group that the changes were designed to improve their understanding of text, but that she would be seeking their input and suggestions for adjusting the procedures along the way. The initial plan agreed upon by Chris and her class for reading instruction included

- reading aloud and taping an assigned text as opposed to only silent reading;
- retelling what they recalled from the text into a tape recorder, then rereading silently;
- completing the comprehension questions after retelling;
- having an RMA conference individually on a biweekly basis with Chris about their miscues and text retellings using the self-analysis sheet found in Appendix D;
- every other week, listening in small CRMA groups to taped readings and retellings and then commenting on the reader's miscues or on the retelling portion of the tape in a responsible, respectful manner;
- concentrating on making personal, life, or textual connections to the readings, regardless of who the reader was; and
- adding details to their comprehension questions as a group that would enhance the connections made to the text.

Student interest was piqued, but the young men were wary of some of the additions to the routine, such as oral reading into a tape player and retelling. It took about a month to complete the cycle with eleven students, particularly since new students were added when others were transferred elsewhere.

These procedures yielded a more flexible instructional approach to reading comprehension improvement for Chris' class while still maintaining a structure with continuous, verifiable assessment and instructional outcomes. While this is not reading workshop as described by Atwell (1998), it is one way of establishing an alternative workshop setting for reading. From RMA reading conferences with Chris to CRMA discussions with peers, there were numerous opportunities for the reader to reread and rethink the text, as well as the connections he was making to it.

Choosing Reading Selections

Previous work in RMA with struggling adolescents taught Chris the importance of selecting interesting, topical readings for the initial miscue analysis with which RMA always begins. Chris chose realistic materials containing conflict, action, and complex characters. Her students, many with criminal records, demanded a sort of no-nonsense realism from their reading. The articles she chose for students to read were written by authors with whom they were familiar. Students preferred nonfiction text, particularly autobiography, biography, and informational narrative, which they often discussed in terms of fact, inference, and the connections they made to "real" stories they could "trust" as people. Many of their CRMA conversations dealt with personal literacy stories directly related to an actual character or event with which they could connect personally or socially.

Implementing the New Plan

Chris distributed copies of short narratives, or expository text, of about four hundred words each dealing with topics such as racism, poverty, abuse, family, and health that were of constant interest and comment within this group of socially and academically at-risk students. Although there was a great deal of student choice in other reading assignments in Chris' class, readings used in RMA conferences and follow-up CRMA were assigned for the sake of having a common text for small-group or teacher-and-student conferences.

Chris altered the otherwise silent reading procedure usually followed in her class. Instead, during the first week of implementation, students took turns tape-recording themselves and listening to their own readings prior to reviewing and answering the comprehension and connection questions. After reading, the students added an unaided retelling to the tape.

After taping, each of the students answered the ten comprehension questions that Chris had prepared earlier. Chris consistently designed at least six of the ten questions with the purpose of helping readers build text-to-text, text-to-self, and text-to-world connections (Keene and Zimmermann 1997; Tovani 2000). For example, to encourage a text-to-text connection, Chris might ask the student to compare a character from a recently read piece with a character in the text the student was currently reading. She often asked text-to-self and text-to-world questions, such as asking the student how he might have responded if he were engaged in a similar conflict (text-to-self) or asking the student to explain a common social, ethical, or moral dilemma represented in a particular article (text-to-life). While answering literal and inferential questions was routine in Chris' classroom, she had not yet formally introduced the idea of making personal or experiential connections to text. Although a bit noisy at first, the students who were taping or listening pragmatically distanced themselves at opposite ends of the classroom.

Sometime during the first and second weeks, Chris marked the miscues on typescripts, selected interesting or revealing miscues for RMA discussion during the reading conference, then examined each of the students' taped retellings for accuracy and detail based on procedures outlined in Goodman and Marek (1996). Chris conferenced individually with students about their high- and low-level miscues of substitution or mispronunciation, vocabulary that was difficult or confusing, dialect and dialogue, meanings or nuances of story, literal versus inferential questions, and how to answer those questions by examining prior knowledge and experiences.

These were RMA conversations between Chris and the reader. For example, Roy read an expository piece about schizophrenia and retold, "This story is about schizophrenic people and how they don't act so much different from normal people and that they do realize they are different from mainstream society." Chris noticed his allusion to mainstream society and followed the retelling with questions about his perceptions of and experiences with mainstream society. The RMA conferences lasted approximately fifteen minutes each—a manageable amount of time with her usual roster. At the time of the reading conference, each student also filled out a self-analysis/feedback form. This was made available for students to take with them to their CRMA session. (See Appendix D.)

Eleven students participated as CRMA partners in small groups every third week to allow Chris to connect lessons with reading discussions and outcomes and to be free to participate as an observer or outside expert during CRMA conversations. They listened to a taped reading and retelling, shared their comprehension and connection questions, and extended the connections they made after listening to other answers. The conversations brought out student reading perceptions, such as Brad's comment: "I'm learning more words that I pick up from these articles but I don't know what I read sometimes." Luke said, "I like short articles on things like gangs, crime, and people—stuff I know more about." Figure 8–1 shows a typical schedule for implementing the new plan, although, as in all classrooms, some degree of flexibility was always maintained.

Week 1	Students read the list of prepared questions. Students tape-record themselves reading text selections. Students listen to themselves read and record an unaided retelling. Students answer the questions on the sheets provided by Chris. Chris marks the miscues on the typescript and selects miscues for RMA discussion during individual reading conferences.
Week 2	Reading conferences (RMA) held between Chris and the students. Students complete self-analysis form (Appendix D).
Week 3	Students hold CRMA group discussions as they listen to and comment on each of the group members' taped readings, retellings, and written answers to comprehension questions. Chris monitors the groups but is not an active participant.
Week 4	The process is repeated.

Figure 8–1. RMA and CRMA Reading Schedule

Documenting Reading Progress

Assessment and documentation of progress are essential to validating reading instruction. Prior to listening to the taped retellings to determine the accuracy, Chris determined a specific number of details or ideas she expected students to conceptualize during the retelling and developed a percentage score for each retelling guide. After looking at numerous examples, Chris fashioned her own retelling guides similar to the retelling guides in Appendices E and F. She then determined how many of the ten comprehension questions were answered adequately, particularly in regard to making strategic connections to self, life, or another text. She charted outcomes for each student every week. The students also documented their progress using the self-analysis/feedback form (Appendix D).

Reading Progress: Brad, Luke, and Roy

As previously stated, attendance in Chris' class fluctuates more than in a traditional high school classroom. For that reason, the reading results and comments from only three students, Brad, Luke, and Roy, who were enrolled for a full semester of CRMA, are included in this chapter. However, a review of the scores of all eleven students suggests overall improvement of all but two of the students who participated. Those two students attended class only twice. Averaged comprehension scores (retellings) for Brad, Luke, and Roy increased by 30 percent. These were measured using protocol sheets similar to those found in Appendices E and F.

Chris found that questioning, rereading, and retelling provided an instructional framework in which readers could connect their personal experiences and knowledge to the text. In the student retellings, she assessed words or phrases that demonstrated students making connections based on personal experiences or knowledge. In the following example, Roy comments on an article dealing with mental health and depression, two problems that persisted in affecting Roy's perceptions of himself:

> This is just about being depressed and how it affects you . . . how the depression illness lasts quite some time. Just all in the way things is . . .

This seventeen-year-old student was frustrated with himself and his personal and academic limitations. He connected to the notion of depression with what Chris interpreted as a personal comment stemming from a defeatist perspective: "Just all in the way things is."

RMA Outcomes: Oral Reading, Making Connections, Empowerment, and Change

The first learning outcome had to do with a greater awareness of the effects of oral reading. Discussion about oral reading prominently emerged during individual conferences and RMA. From individual conferences as well as RMA conversations, Chris learned that oral reading of text retained its place as an important part of what the students were learning about themselves as readers. One of the things they were interested in was how the reader "sounded." Reading with expression and enthusiasm was important to these students because it represented empowerment to them. It was not about being fluent at all costs, which is what often narrowly defines reading; rather, it was about their already fragile self-esteem and an unspoken desire by many of them to fit into what was normal and mainstream. This was a goal the students had not yet figured out how to attain, or else they would not have been remanded to this alternative high school setting.

Chris encouraged the readers to examine the overall effects of the new reading approach on their reading confidence and progress, resulting in the following comments. These comments proved useful in Chris' instructional decision making. Luke said it helped his understanding if, after audiotaping the text, he listened to himself read on tape before answering the prepared questions. Roy noted that reading aloud is "harder but it's good to hear yourself" because it improves pronunciation and voice quality; and Brad said that reading aloud "helped build a better vocabulary." These perceptions consistently emerged in the course of CRMA conversations as well as the RMA conferences with Chris.

The second outcome had to do with making connections to text. Besides individual taping followed by conferencing with Chris, twice a month a small group of three or four students during CRMA listened to a portion of each reader's tape and, selecting from their copies of the RMA organizer used in the earlier reading conference, commented on the reader, the miscues, the retelling, and the process in general. Chris asked that they carefully listen for and comment on ways the reader made connections to the text. Although the conversations were a bit weak at first, Chris noted from her observations of these groups that by the last two sessions, there were many connections made to personal experiences, either affirming the text or discounting its reality. They expected realism and validation for their lives in classroom experiences, particularly reading, and when the reading did not conform to their experiences, interests, and perceptions, comments such as "This ain't the way this would go down in my neighborhood," or "This is about potato packaging and how dirty potatoes don't sell. I don't know . . . " would emerge.

Third, during the CRMA discussions, the students were empowered participants in the process. They discussed how this new approach to reading was working and what could be improved. Chris, roving from one group to another, noted and validated their comments. For example, during the first month of RMA, since the students were not typically expected to retell after reading in class, they expressed frustration. Even though she had previously demonstrated the various steps, this one needed further clarification. Chris commented, "I did not want to confine the students' thinking, so I tried to explain it [retelling] as summarizing or including information from the beginning, middle, and end of the story." The second month of RMA discussions revealed that retellings still caused frustration and needed yet more explanation.

Chris explained, "My next description to them was to tell the information into the tape recorder as if it were a person (say, the teacher for your next class). I offered to sit and let them tell me (while recording) about what they had just read." The students remained uncomfortable with the process, so Chris turned to them for a solution. One student suggested that prereading, but not answering, the comprehension questions made the retelling easier. The class agreed and this became a part of the routine. Chris also heard several students express difficulty retaining the information to retell. She recommended that before recording the retelling, they reread portions of the text and try to include those points when relating their version. This was well received and successful. As before, although not a requirement, these modifications became a part of the RMA process. Chris saw steady gains in both comprehension and retelling scores shortly after these changes took place. The modified routine eased anxiety about retelling and allowed more information to emerge, some of which went well beyond the scope of the prepared comprehension questions.

In addition to commenting on retelling concerns, students also said that Chris needed to reinforce the idea that comments from CRMA group members should be constructive and focused on the text, not because there were existing discussion problems, but because the students were unsure of how to proceed during the discussion. They demonstrated their willingness to fit into the CRMA group when given satisfactory direction. Chris added, "They were really taking this seriously, except for a few nervous giggles and jabs."

As a result of Chris' observations, class conversations, and student input, the final instructional approach was modified to include (1) reading and recording the selection prior to silent reading, (2) reading the comprehension questions and thinking about them in relationship to the text, (3) retelling the story in chunks, that is, retelling as much as possible, then rereading portions of the text to gain greater understanding, (4) biweekly reading conferences with Chris guided by the reader, and (5) monthly CRMA group discussions to comment constructively on each of the group members' reading and retelling with emphasis on making real-life connections to the text.

The Power of RMA and CRMA with Struggling Adolescent Learners

As we have emphasized throughout this book, the intent and importance of RMA as an instructional method is to move the reader toward understanding and valuing his own knowledge of language instead of having the reader give up on ever being able to read proficiently. Revaluing the reader's voice, knowledge, and experiences while empowering him to value himself through the examination of his own reading process was more important to Chris than any other part of this project. Brad's comment from the beginning of this chapter does not refer to the kind of material read but the actual reading miscues that may occur, whether orally or silently, that change the meaning of the text. As discussed in previous chapters, RMA invites the reader to analyze and view miscues as attempts to construct meaning, rather than perceive them as failed attempts to learn. It represents a metacognitive process in which the reader must think about what she is thinking when the miscue occurs.

Discussing and valuing reading miscues as ways of understanding how each reader transacts with text (Rosenblatt 1978) guides readers toward considering their own ideas and perceptions about reading and other matters in a socially acceptable and healthy way—something important to the students in Chris' class. Dialogue during RMA, whether in a one-on-one conference with the teacher or in CRMA groups, is designed to empower learners to "define themselves as readers: literate human beings capable of learning what they want to learn" (Goodman and Marek 1996, 203). We believe this concept is important to all ages but critical to troubled adolescents who are trying to find their place in the world.

Summing It Up and Moving On

From previous experience, Chris was certain that the process of RMA contains elements of practice that have the potential to serve readers in vocabulary, decoding, and comprehension, depending upon student learning needs. Students who had proficient decoding skills but did not comprehend the text were becoming more and more common in Chris' classroom, just as they are in other, more typical language arts and reading settings (Garan 2002). She sought to focus on two things: (1) modifying the RMA retelling process to aid comprehension connections between text, self, and the world and (2) involving students in decisions related to making these modifications.

The teacher-prepared questions that prompted the readers to build reading connections to the text provided excellent scaffolding tools. These were not published worksheets but teacher-created instructional tools customized to meet the evolving needs of the students in Chris' classroom. The influence of these questions was not apparent until after the first retelling session, during which time the students suggested reading the questions first, then retelling the text as they remembered it, similar to the concept of guided retelling. As a result of implementing this suggestion, the retellings were richer and more connected to individual personalities and knowledge.

Three of the student learning outcomes we have discussed added considerable information to the understanding of RMA. First is the idea that oral reading is more than reading the text. According to adolescent students, it can increase understanding, vocabulary, and pronunciation. Second, when the reading is carefully scaffolded through retelling, conferences, and guiding questions, struggling readers can make strong personal, social, and textual connections to what they read. And, finally, the students clearly demonstrated the importance of being involved in the decision-making process of RMA and CRMA implementation. They helped Chris realize that RMA and CRMA should be continuously monitored to maximize utility to the learner. Empowered, the students took charge of the process and carried out the expectations they had all agreed upon.

9

Frequently Asked Questions About RMA and CRMA

This chapter will

- provide answers to a variety of frequently asked questions about RMA and CRMA;
- suggest ways that RMA can be used within the classroom as an instructional process; and
- discuss the benefits of RMA and CRMA.

General Questions About RMA and CRMA

Proposing new ideas in literacy education, particularly in today's world of strict accountability, is risky. Many questions arise when adopting a new reading methodology and instruction. To support the use of RMA and CRMA, we answer questions that are frequently asked of us about these related strategies.

What is the most common pitfall in RMA?

Sometimes teachers want to hear only what *they* consider focused and meaningful responses during RMA. That happened to Karen as her RMA group (Nathan, Steve, and Justin) listened to Nathan's previously taped miscue session and Nathan corrected his reading of "skit shirt" to "silk scarf." Rita and Karen tried unsuccessfully to help him see this as a semantic correction rather than one related to a phonics rule about *r*-controlled vowels. Nathan wanted to explain how he figured out *scarf*, saying that "the *ar* is an *r*-controlled vowel," and his teacher should have asked him to explain what he knew about the rule. Justin was also quietly trying to discuss what he had determined to be a smart, or high-level, miscue, but that was lost in the teacher's attempt to stay with her own agenda.

TEACHER: Great! You just corrected yourself. How do you know that it's *silk scarf*?

NATHAN: We, uh, learned about *r*-controlled vowels in class and . . .

TEACHER: Does it make sense to wear a skirt around your neck?

NATHAN: No . . . (*giggles*)

TEACHER: What do you think was in your brain when you said "skirt" for *scarf*?

NATHAN: *-Ar* means an *r*-controlled vowel.

JUSTIN: He said "loose" for *loosely*. I think that's a smart miscue . . .

Karen was not paying close attention to what Justin and Nathan were saying about making their own learning connections. Nathan had just learned about *r*-controlled vowels in his regular classroom. This knowledge emerged in the form of a phonics rule and, although it did not help him with meaning, he did apply his knowledge as a pronunciation strategy. And Justin, who had earlier evidenced difficulty with the concept of smart miscues, had found one. The trick to keeping RMA discussions on track is really listening to what the participants are saying about their miscues. This takes practice since the teacher is listening to students in a different way than in typical classroom curriculum interactions.

How long will it take to learn miscue analysis so I can conduct RMA?

Not as long as you might think. For example, most teachers know how to conduct running records (Clay 2000), the markings of which are similar to miscue analysis. Most teachers, particularly reading specialists, know how to administer an informal reading inventory, a number of which now include a section on the analysis of miscues. Chapter 3 provides a step-by-step guide to support miscue analysis.

Questions About RMA and CRMA in the Classroom

How can RMA or CRMA be scheduled into a regular classroom routine such as guided reading or reading conferences?

Ongoing classroom or resource room RMA conversations may be scheduled into reading time one to three times a week, depending on how adept the RMA partners are in carrying out the process. They may also be scheduled into conferences or reading discussions, as seen in Chris' language arts classroom in Chapter 8. The number and type of RMA conversations scheduled depends largely upon teacher resources, student need, and class size. A teacher may use conversation around a student's miscue to shape a reading conference. Or CRMA groups may meet alternately with literature circle groups—one centers around the reader and one around the text; however, the voice of the reader is validated in each setting. There may also be overlap in topics discussed: students in literature circles may reflect on connections or questions they have about retelling or a miscue that affected understanding. In almost any reading event, the teacher could use many of the RMA questions to extend and expand thinking surrounding topics that students have generated. For example, in Vicki's classroom during literature circle conversations, students are asked to make personal, textual, and social connections to texts just as they do in CRMA.

Guided reading provides a natural structure for RMA conversations. When Karen visited other classrooms, she noticed the guided reading discussions were teacher directed and there was no discussion about oral miscues that helped students conceptualize the reading process as one of predicting and confirming information based on the reader's prior knowledge. The interactive piece of social involvement and comment by peers on miscue choices and the reading process in general was missing. As a result, Karen reorganized *follow-up* guided reading sessions in her Title I classrooms to reflect her knowledge of and experiences with RMA.

As with guided reading, Karen facilitated conversations on reading and comprehension strategies in her small classrooms. Unlike guided reading in the regular classroom, these conversations included a simple analysis of miscues and retellings as the children read aloud or retold the text. This approach utilizes familiar aspects of guided reading but with an emphasis on student-led discussion about the reading process.

Figure 9–1 shows a step-by-step procedure Karen used to implement RMA into the guided reading sessions she was required to conduct.

A great deal has been learned about guided reading procedures (Pinnell and Fountas 2000) as strategies for helping children become stronger readers, but the element of student response to miscues is not a part of the published guided reading

Step 1:	Students gather with their guided reading selections.
Step 2:	Using a quiet voice, each student reads aloud while Karen listens and circles miscues on her text copy with the child's initials.
Step 3:	Karen discusses with the group if the miscue made sense and if it changed the meaning after the reader finishes.
Step 4:	Karen moves on to listen to another reader and repeats steps 1–3.
Step 5:	Karen gathers the group together for a group retelling of the story.
Step 6:	Karen discusses selected miscues she noticed and invites the reader who miscued to comment.
Step 7:	Karen invites other reading group participants to discuss why they think the reader miscued.

Figure 9–1. Supporting Guided Reading Instruction with RMA

process. Like Karen, we believe that guided reading should involve more than listening to children read, helping them problem solve words, and discussing context. If the goal of guided reading is to "assist children in becoming independent, fluent, silent readers" (Fawson and Reutzel 2000, 85), then RMA and CRMA should be included.

Guided reading strategies coupled with RMA strategies empower the readers in Karen's resource room classes to use their miscues to construct meaning and strengthen their understanding of the strategies that make them good readers. As a result, overall student attitudes and conceptualizations of reading have changed. For example, one day, a group of Karen's third-grade students were taking turns reading aloud for fun. One reader made a high-level miscue but one of the other students insisted on correcting her. Another student, who was familiar with RMA from previous work with Karen, looked squarely at the *corrector* and said, "It's a smart miscue. It doesn't change the meaning." Interestingly, a few days later, the same corrector encouraged another student who had miscued and stopped, with some uncertainty, to reread his miscue. The corrector said, "It's OK, keep reading, it's a smart miscue." Karen facilitated conversations about high-level miscues in both instances—an occurrence that most likely would not happen in a classroom where time spent in guided reading did not include RMA questions and procedures.

Are there common questions that guide RMA discussions?

To guide the RMA discussion, whether it is in a collaborative group (CRMA) or between teacher and student, the reader and the conversation partner(s) together discuss the reader's miscues by questioning: (1) if the miscue made sense, (2) if it changed the meaning of the sentence, and (3) why the reader miscued. It is helpful to write these questions, and others you may wish to ask, on the RMA organizer or even keep them posted in the classroom.

It is also helpful to question the type of miscue made in order to name the reading strategy used. For example, it is important to know if it was a miscue of substitution in which the reader used a placeholder to keep going or if the reader omitted the word and picked it up later in the text. These kinds of distinctions keep the RMA partners focused on what the reader knows and what she did to make the miscue. Although the discussion may vary with the readers, using these questions helps guide the reader toward discovering that "just as authors make decisions on how to create meaning in their stories, readers, too, make those decisions for themselves" toward the goal of "constructing a meaningful text" (Strickland and Strickland 2000, 55).

With older students, the conversation may focus less on miscues and more on retelling and comprehension; therefore, some sort of focusing technique is useful.

For example, Chris, the high school language arts teacher, emphasizes personal and intertextual connections as springboards into discussing how readers might develop richer retellings by consciously making these connections to text and talking about them. This is especially helpful if the student reads with fluency but comprehends little.

How do I involve proficient readers in RMA or CRMA?

Vicki, a fifth-grade teacher, asked six of her proficient readers to discuss on videotape some of their responses from the Burke Interview, particularly in regard to reading strategies they use for unknown vocabulary, what they do when the text is too difficult, how they make connections to what they read, and how they became strong readers. She ended with asking them what advice they would give to a reader who is still sounding out words. Readers enjoy analyzing their miscues and figuring out how language works. This is just as rewarding and enriching a process for proficient readers as it is for those who struggle.

I'm still confused: What is CRMA?

As detailed in Chapter 6, CRMA is a collaborative effort among students assigned to small groups to discuss miscues and retellings without the continuous or direct facilitation of a teacher. CRMA may be conducted with readers with a range of reading proficiencies, with a group who struggles, or with a group with high reading proficiencies. We have found that CRMA works best with intermediate to high school readers; however, that should not discourage teachers from trying this strategy with younger readers. The structure of CRMA conversations varies with student learning needs.

CRMA is flexible in that oral miscues, the retellings, or both may guide the conversation. With some high school readers, Chris discovered that oral miscues may not be the most useful or interesting focus of the CRMA conversation; rather, the retelling of the text, the number of details retold, and the degree of comprehension might be more appropriate and interesting to this age group.

Questions About the Benefits of RMA and CRMA

What are the benefits of RMA over other reading methods and strategies?

During RMA conversations, the reader is invited to reflectively examine and value reading miscues as evidence of logical attempts to make sense from text, based on prior knowledge as well as an understanding of how language works. Through this strategic dialogue, the reader begins to understand the reading process, build proficiency in reading comprehension by focusing on meaning rather than only on fluency, and improve his self-confidence as a learner (Worsnop 1996). In essence, RMA seeks to empower readers to view reading miscues as repeated attempts to predict meaning and to make sense of text. RMA encourages and empowers the reader to identify and build on reading strengths. Ideally, RMA conversations lead to the discovery and practice of new and varied reading strategies that, through strategic conversations, the reader selects and defines.

RMA conversations open doors for collaborative discussion and greater reading success as readers examine some of the factors affecting reading proficiency. Struggling readers, particularly older students, may have given up on themselves as learners because they believe they were not born with the same abilities to learn as others. These conversations provide them with the opportunity to see themselves in a very different light.

What are some specific benefits of RMA that I can share with parents and administrators who may be skeptical?

RMA methodology is inexpensive and well researched. Teachers need only typescripts, markers, and audiotaping equipment. RMA is a powerful form of professional development for teachers who wish to learn more about the reading process. RMA can involve not only teachers and students but paraprofessionals, volunteers, and parents as well. Many school districts and schools of education are encouraging teachers to conduct action research projects, and the RMA process is highly adaptable to action research procedures, as Karen demonstrated in working with Nathan (Moore 2003).

Direct benefits include strengthening the reader's repertoire of effective reading strategies as well as offering students a safe forum for learning when miscues are disrupting meaning making. Bringing reading to a conscious level encourages readers to be more receptive to the use of proficient reading strategies. And most important to administrators and parents: reading results happen quickly. They are easily documented through ongoing miscue analysis and retelling guides (see Appendices E and F). The teacher does not have to construct elaborate rubrics to document the assessment.

If the RMA process is implemented as a part of the classroom routine and students consistently participate, then reading achievement will improve. We have found specifically that vocabulary and comprehension are most affected by RMA. The gains made by students in this book are real and well documented. We also recommend the research of Ken Goodman (1996b), Yetta Goodman and Ann Marek (1996), Prisca Martens (1998), Dorothy Watson (1978, 1996a, 1996b), and Ruth Davenport (1993, 2002). Each of these experts has authored books and/ or articles on the successful use of RMA. (See Appendix H for a summary of the research on RMA.)

What kinds of learners benefit most from RMA or CRMA?

While all students may benefit from RMA, teachers may wish to schedule only some of their readers into RMA or CRMA groups. Generally, we have found that students who benefit the most are those who do not conceptualize reading as a meaning-making process. Like Justin, Devon, and Matt, these students generally do not understand themselves as readers; therefore, they often limit their reading strategies to sounding it out. Or, like some of Chris' students, they may not make connections to, nor understand, what they are reading even though they may read with fluency.

Do second language learners also benefit from RMA?

Students who are English language learners (ELLs) may approach RMA a little differently because two languages are involved, but the benefits are evident. Bev, a teacher in a rural school with a large Latino population, asks her ELL students to read text in both English and Spanish. (There are a number of free translation websites available to expedite this.) She encourages reading in both the first and the second language because the first language often supports reading comprehension in the second one. She then marks the miscues on the English text to discuss differences in language pronunciation as well as whether the miscue makes sense in that language. She also conducts retellings in both English and Spanish. For the English retelling, Bev added drawing to help students understand English. She found that having the reader draw responses *while* she retells supports and enhances comprehension in English as well as in Spanish. Although Matt, one of Jennifer's students, was not an ELL student, he also used drawing as a strategy as he retold to help him remember the story.

What factors affect the processes, procedures, and outcomes of RMA and CRMA?

Factors that affect RMA processes, procedures, and outcomes are age and maturity, motivation, interests, perceptions of learning, level of responsibility, trust, cultural background, language background, and reading ability. For example, Jennifer, Karen, Vicki, and Chris found they had to clarify student perceptions of learning before gaining student trust in the RMA process. That trust and understanding led to successful RMA outcomes. When working with two struggling seventh-grade readers, Jennifer found that trust could be gained through RMA sessions (teacher and student), then extended to collaborative (CRMA) sessions between the teacher and the students.

Variations in reading ability also affect RMA outcomes. Not all students' reading abilities are equal. Some readers may miscue repeatedly but still relate a reasonably comprehensive retelling. Readers who appear fluent may not be proficient in comprehending text or they may miss the meaning entirely, thus creating their own version of the story during retelling. For both types of readers, critical discussions about their own miscues (in the oral reading or in retellings) may eventually equip them with greater skill in using a broad range of reading strategies to acquire greater meaning from text.

Summing It Up and Moving On

In this chapter we have addressed common questions that teachers have about RMA and CRMA. Both are instructional procedures that rely on the knowledge and decision-making skills of the teacher implementing them. They are flexible enough to fit into the regular reading curriculum and address special needs. We emphasize that the questions and discussions associated with RMA and CRMA carry over into instructional procedures in a positive, supportive manner because students use exploratory talk to further their understanding of their reading and learning processes.

10

Reflections on Assessment, Teaching, and Learning Through RMA

This chapter will

- • reflect on RMA as an authentic assessment and instructional process and
- • emphasize the connection between assessment and instruction.

Love, Your Good Reader, Justin

We have found that explaining RMA as an assessment and instructional tool through the stories of children makes the most sense to those of us who are teachers. One of our favorite stories follows; it illustrates how assessment links to instruction.

When Karen first introduced Rita to Justin, he was a quiet, struggling reader who described himself as a "kinda bad" reader, but he loved baseball, being with friends, and watching movies. This polite, socially well adjusted fourth-grade student was on his way to being referred to special education largely because his score on an IQ test was borderline and he was failing reading in the regular classroom. Karen was Justin's Title I reading teacher. Worried that he might be headed toward the wrong placement, she asked if RMA might bring out Justin's strengths and give him greater confidence. After visiting with Justin, hearing him read aloud, and reviewing his answers to the Burke Reading Interview (see Appendix A), it was obvious to us that he did not belong in special education classes. His choppy reading was not as troublesome as was his low confidence in himself as a reader. He was very reluctant to talk about what he read.

We decided to place Justin in an RMA group with two other struggling readers, Nathan and Steve. Justin's confidence gradually increased. By having him listen to his taped readings while following along with the text, Karen demonstrated to him that repetition was one of his more effective reading strategies. When she explained that he was simply checking for meaning, Justin showed surprise.

Though Justin had a basic knowledge of reading—he knew how to sound out the words and that text was supposed to make sense—he was literally afraid to trust his own reading instincts. For example, at first, he considered substitution not as a strategy for gaining meaning but as "messing up," and he was embarrassed about each substitution. His attention to the text's meaning was doomed because he feared failure. With help from his RMA partners, Justin learned to understand what he was reading by making connections to the text and to recognize that repetition and substitution can be helpful reading strategies. This assessment was shared with his classroom teacher so that she could modify instruction for Justin as well.

After only ten RMA sessions, Justin independently explained why he miscued, and if the miscues altered the meaning, he self-corrected with enthusiasm. Justin's confidence soared. He proudly demonstrated his newfound facility with vocabulary and he often made sophisticated connections between texts. During RMA conversations, Karen and Rita learned that his metacognitive vocabulary reasoning skills were quite strong—something no one else had discovered previously.

Justin's motivation to read grew when he realized he was capable of reading interesting chapter books. Near the end of the school year, Rita asked him to send her an email listing titles of books he had recently read. His email was signed "Love, your good reader, Justin." By the end of the school year, Justin had a B in reading in his regular classroom and was no longer being considered for special education referral. His perceptions of himself as a reader had changed drastically. His parents were pleased, as was his classroom teacher, who remarked to Karen, "I don't know what you did but it sure worked for Justin!" Karen shared some of the questioning strategies associated with RMA conversations with Justin's teacher, hoping that she would begin to find ways of incorporating these into her work with Justin. Justin moved on to middle school two years later, not as a failure, but as a good reader.

Assessment Leads and Informs Instruction

Assessing RMA responses leads to instructional action. Closely examining what a reader does naturally leads teachers to better instructional decision making. Karen, in her Title I reading classes, constructed minilessons on everything from phonics to think-alouds based on her students' RMA conversation results (Moore and Brantingham 2003). Regular and retrospective analysis of reader miscues signifies what Chris termed "reflective conversations and mindful considerations of the reading process" (Moore and Aspegren 2001, 502). When Chris worked with Dan, a high school senior, she learned that his vocabulary was limited primarily by his reading ability when he said, "I know about a lot, but sometimes can't read the words that go with it." RMA teaches us what readers know as well as where they need the greatest support.

Students learn to assess their own responses during RMA. When Nathan, a fourth-grade reader, determined that the use of placeholders in reading was a bridge between fluency and understanding, his miscues became approachable and useful as learning tools. Matt, a seventh grader, noted that choice in what he read helped him become a better reader. Brad, a high school senior, found his comprehension increased when he read short news articles about real-life events. All of these student insights informed further instruction.

In addition to assessing student learning and directing instructional decisions, RMA may also affect the teacher's outlook on assessment, teaching, and learning. Assessment of the RMA conversation ultimately affects the teacher's instructional choices and practice in teaching reading; however, since RMA demands a different way of looking at student response, the theory behind the process often spills over into other aspects of the curriculum. Chris and Karen, as well as other teachers contributing to this book, said it represented a turning point in the way they viewed the relationship between teaching, assessment, and learning.

Chris noted that as she grew more skilled in using RMA, she found herself routinely using the concept of constructively exploring unexpected learner responses in a broader context within her language arts and reading classroom. In effect, she viewed miscues as new opportunities for better understanding the thinking processes of her students both within and outside of RMA or CRMA conversations.

Assessment is not limited to student behaviors. Karen often referred to what she learned from ineffective teaching actions, which she called "teaching miscues." Part of the assessment and instruction process is listening carefully to what the RMA participants are trying to explain rather than listening for what teachers want to hear them say. Karen videotapes RMA sessions so that she can monitor her own teaching behaviors. She explains, "Until I started taping and reviewing reading lessons, I did not realize how much I *led* the reader. I was doing all the talking!"

Assessment links instruction to learning theory. In RMA we explore the social interactive theory of Vygotsky (1978) and the sociolinguistic theory of Halliday (1980) as well as empowerment issues. Jennifer introduced us to the entity theory of learning, in which students believe that learning is innate (Dweck and Bempechet 1983). In other words, if you are not born with the ability to read, then why bother to struggle? She found that struggling learners, especially adolescents labeled learning disabled, often try to sabotage the instructional process when they are beginning to do well because in their view it is impossible for them to succeed. It is better to undermine the progress than accept a different perspective on their learning. Jennifer found the way to get past that view was demonstration on the teacher's part and a gradual shift of responsibility to the students. Based on her assessment of what the two boys she was working with *could* do, she developed a plan of action that gradually empowered them to discuss their miscues and to finally realize they had reading strengths. Eventually, they were able to work through text together.

RMA is more than an activity or routine assessment of skills for teachers and students. Instead, it is a way of thinking about teaching and learning. Throughout this book, we have demonstrated how RMA connects assessment and instruction. RMA offers a research-based teaching and learning alternative that impacts choice of teaching action, materials, and classroom routines. Instead of relying on expensive, sometimes ineffective, scripted texts, reading activities, or assessments, the RMA process directly involves and empowers students and teachers in *conversations* about reading. These conversations lead directly to authentic assessment and instruction that empowers the reader, validates student voice, and provides myriad opportunities for reading success.

Running Record Typescript and RMA Organizer for Nathan

Following are two lines from a reading and the RMA session organizer for those lines.

Running Record

Line	Text					
001	Mr. Davis is a beekeeper.	✓	~~Davs~~ Davis	✓	✓	✓
002	His first job every morning	✓	✓	✓	✓	✓
003	is to check the hives.	✓	✓	✓	his / the	✓
004	The hives are different colors.	✓	✓	✓	✓	✓
005	Bees can recognize colors.	✓	✓	recrise / reconize / recognize	✓

RMA Organizer for Nathan

Line	Text	Miscue as Read	Graph. (b/m/e)	Syn.	Sem.	Mng. Chng.	C
001	Davis	Davs	b/m/e	y	y	n	n
003	the	his	-/-/-	y	y	n	n
005	recognize	recrise	b/-/e	y	n	—	n
		reconize	b/-/e	y	n	—	n

Notice that each one of Nathan's attempts for *recognize* is recorded and marked *y* under Syntax because, even though they are nonwords, their endings (-ize and -ise) are similar to that of the verb *recognize*, indicating that the reader was using knowledge of syntax to construct a placeholder for the correct word.

Appendix H

A Summary of the Research

Having a sound research base from which to teach has always been necessary for quality instruction. In today's climate of accountability, it is more important than ever to be able to cite the research and theory behind our practice. For that reason, we have written a short summary of the research supporting RMA.

Retrospective miscue analysis is grounded in extensive reading miscue analysis research that began with the work of Ken Goodman (1968, 1969) and continued through his ongoing research (1996a) and that of others (see Alan and Watson 1977; Bloome and Dail 1997; Goodman, Watson, and Burke 1987, 2005; Goodman 1995; Martens 1998; and Watson 1996a, 1996b). RMA is rooted in linguistic research rather than reductionist, or skills-based, research, in which decoding text correctly and in sequence is the primary focus of reading instruction (Goodman 1994). Linguistic researchers "consider reading as an active, receptive language process and readers as users of language" (Goodman 1994, 1096).

Research into the analysis of oral reading miscues demonstrates that "miscues are unexpected responses cued by the reader's knowledge of his or her language and concepts of the world. . . . when expected and unexpected responses match, we get few insights into this process. When they do not match and a miscue results, teachers as researchers have a 'window' on the reading process" (Goodman 1973, 5). For the purpose of informing instructional practice, the teacher may look for patterns in these mismatches to document what readers know about the pragmatic and semantic (meaning), syntactic (grammar), and graphophonic (letter-sound association) language cueing systems (Goodman 1996a; Weaver 1994) and how they use that knowledge to make sense of text. More recently, educators like Wilde (2000) and Davenport (2002) have published versions of miscue analysis to fit into reading workshop or to use as data for reading conferences with the intent of building on student strengths and helping teachers better understand students as readers. RMA is different only in that it directly involves the student in making decisions about and investigating his own miscues. The information the teacher learns about the reader comes from the miscue analysis and the RMA discussions. Teachers who are interested in more information about miscue analysis may wish to consult *Reading Miscue Inventory: Alternative Procedures* (Goodman, Watson, and Burke 1987),

Reading Miscue Inventory: From Evaluation to Instruction for All Readers (Goodman, Watson, and Burke 2005), *Miscue Analysis Made Easy* (Wilde 2000), and/or *Miscues Not Mistakes* (Davenport 2002).

RMA is strongly linked to the research in sociopsycholinguistics, which reveals intricate connections between the social, cognitive, and linguistic aspects of reading and language development. During RMA conversations, readers are invited to make social, personal, and cognitive connections to text to better understand the reading and language processes. Once they understand what really happens as they read, they are empowered to make decisions about their own interpretations of meaning. Consider this metaphor: How do you learn to ride a bicycle if you have no knowledge of what it means to ride a bike? Reading works the same way. One of the best ways to help children understand the reading process is to engage them in discussion about their reading miscues and retellings, providing them with evidence of the language process at work.

Extensive miscue analysis and RMA research demonstrates that reading is not simply a process of decoding, although decoding is integral to the process. The research clearly demonstrates to teachers and students what readers *do* when they read: they take their background knowledge and apply it to all they know about language as they predict and confirm the meaning of the text. Goodman (1973) suggests they create parallel texts to the author's text. Davenport (2002) explains:

> While a reader is trying to understand what the author is saying, she is building her own meaning, which will always vary slightly from the author's intended meaning. This personally-constructed text governs what the reader perceives and the syntax that is assigned to what is read. As the reader is constructing both the structure and meaning of the text, sometimes the text in the reader's head must be reconstructed to maintain meaning. (13)

Some readers need more help than others in figuring out the reading process. RMA gives readers the opportunity to do so as they examine patterns in their miscues such as substitutions, omissions, insertions, and placeholders. These patterns provide evidence that they are using their knowledge of language to create meaning from text.

Retrospective miscue analysis draws on a variety of research: the value of classroom talk (Barnes [1975] 1992; Barnes, Britton, and Rosen 1969; Barnes, Britton, and Torbe 1990; Wells 1986; Wells and Chang-Wells 1992); social interaction (Goodman 1996a; Vygotsky 1978); and learner empowerment issues (Christian and Bloome 2005; Gore 1993). Also informing RMA is Rosenblatt's work (1978) exploring how readers transact with text not as a one-way exchange between author and reader but as a two-way transaction in which the reader actively engages in creating meaning from text. RMA is strongly linked to research in sociopsycholinguistics, which reveals intricate connections between the social, cognitive, and linguistic aspect of reading and language development (Lindfors 1991; Smith 1994; Weaver 1994).

The use of RMA by teachers originated from a process called *reader-selected miscues* (RSM), developed by Dorothy Watson to spark classroom discussions about reading among junior high students (Watson 1978; Watson and Hoge 1996). In RSM, readers select words that troubled them during silent reading and then discuss those miscues with a teacher or a small group. Later, Worsnop worked with struggling adolescent readers (1980), and Marek (1987) conducted her dissertation research with a troubled adult reader named Gina. Marek's research was then used as the foundation for developing a study on the effectiveness of using RMA with seventh graders (Goodman and Flurkey 1996). In each of these studies, struggling readers gained greater understanding of the reading process and became more confident, fluent readers. Improvement in reading grades and increased interest in leisure reading were also noted.

RMA is an approach to reading assessment and instruction originally published by Goodman and Marek (1996) as a reading strategy for middle school and older readers. RMA has been reflected in the work of many researchers who conducted studies with teachers and particularly puzzling, struggling readers (Goodman and Marek 1996; Martens 1998; Moore and Aspegren 2001; Moore and Brantingham 2003). In each of these studies, word recognition and comprehension scores improved dramatically and fluency improvement followed. In addition, teachers using RMA developed a much better understanding of what readers *do* when they read as they listened carefully to (1) graphophonic patterns in oral reading, (2) syntactic patterns in oral reading, and (3) semantic patterns both in oral reading and in retelling of text.

Research in RMA has grown to include readers in the elementary grades. Through the work of researchers such as Gilles and Dickinson (2000), Martens (1998), and Moore and Brantingham (2003), we are beginning to understand how RMA works with developing readers. In her dissertation work, Folger (2001) looked at text construction with readers participating in retrospective miscue analysis. She found that readers used their knowledge of language at word, sentence, and story levels to make connections to their own experiences and in visualizing and constructing parallel texts. Her results are consistent with what researchers using RMA with older readers have asserted: students moved away from relying solely on phonetic decoding, they became more metacognitive about their reading process, and they showed an increase in strategy use. Building on our knowledge about early readers, a recent study by Pahls-Weiss (2002) conducted in an early childhood setting examined the effects of using RMA with first-grade students. Pahls-Weiss, too, found that first-grade students who participated in RMA began to take a more analytical approach to reading, increased their use of the syntactic and semantic cueing systems, and decreased repetitions, indicating more efficient reading. This growing body of research suggests that regardless of age, RMA helps readers become more efficient and effective.

Collaborative RMA in small groups is a relatively new and unexplored concept in reading research, originating with the doctoral work of Costello (1992, 1996), who wanted to see how small groups of struggling middle school readers with a range of proficiencies would talk together about reading miscues. Costello's work is a bit different than what we propose. In her model, the teacher's role was to mediate and interpret what middle school students thought they were saying or thinking when they miscued. The focus for her students was on oral reading miscues while we include retelling as a part of both the RMA and the CRMA process. Research on CRMA remains ongoing.

Research in the area of RMA and CRMA is dynamic and fluid. As an assessment and instructional tool, it is opening more windows on the reading and learning processes for teachers and students alike.

References

Alan, P., and D. J. Watson. 1977. *Findings of Research in Miscue Analysis: Classroom Implications*. Urbana, IL: ERIC and National Council of Teachers of English.

Atwell, N. 1998. *In the Middle: New Understandings About Writing, Reading, and Learning*. 2d ed. Portsmouth, NH: Boynton/Cook.

Barnes, D. [1975] 1992. *From Communication to Curriculum*. London: Penguin.

Barnes, D. R., J. Britton, and H. Rosen. 1969. *Language, the Learner, and the School*. London: Penguin.

Barnes, D. R., J. Britton, and M. Torbe. 1990. *Language, the Learner, and the School*. 4th ed. Portsmouth, NH: Boynton/Cook.

Bloome, D., and A. R. K. Dail. 1997. "Toward (Re)Defining Miscue Analysis: Reading as a Social and Cultural Process." *Language Arts* 74 (8): 610–17.

Blumenfeld, P. C., and R. W. Marx. 1997. "Motivation and Cognition." In *Multiple Perspective Analysis of Classroom Discourse*, ed. H. J. Walberg and G. D. Haertel, 79–106. Norwood, NJ: Ablex.

Burke, C. 1987. "Reading Interview." In *Reading Miscue Inventory: Alternative Procedures*, ed. Y. M. Goodman, D. J. Watson, and C. L. Burke, 219. New York: Richard C. Owen.

Christian, B., and C. Bloome. 2005. "Learning to Read Is Who You Are." *Reading and Writing Quarterly* 20 (4): 365–84.

Clay, M. M. 2000. *Running Records for Classroom Teachers*. Portsmouth, NH: Heinemann.

Costello, S. 1992. Collaborative Retrospective Miscue Analysis with Middle School Students. Doctoral diss., University of Arizona.

———. 1996. "A Teacher Researcher Uses RMA." In *Retrospective Miscue Analysis: Revaluing Readers and Reading*, ed. Y. M. Goodman and A. M. Marek, 165–75. Katonah, NY: Richard C. Owen.

Covington, M. 1983. "Motivated Cognitions." In *Learning and Motivation in the Classroom*, ed. S. Paris, B. Olson, and H. Stevenson, 139–64. Hillsdale, NJ: Lawrence Erlbaum.

Cricinfo, W. 2004. "Twenty20 Ashes Clash Gets Boards' Approval." In *Cricket News*. *http://aus.cricinfo.com/db/ARCHIVE/CRICKET_NEWS/2004/JUN/165724_ ENG_09JUN2004.html*.

Davenport, M. R. 1993. "Reflecting Through Talk on Content Area Reading." In *Cycles of Meaning: Exploring the Potential of Talk in Learning Communities*, ed. K. M. Pierce and C. Gilles, 179–96. Portsmouth, NH: Heinemann.

———. 2002. *Miscues Not Mistakes: Reading Assessment in the Classroom*. Portsmouth, NH: Heinemann.

Dweck, C., and J. Bempechet. 1983. "Children's Theories of Intelligence: Consequences for Learning." In *Learning and Motivation in the Classroom*, ed. S. Paris, B. Olson, and H. Stevenson, 239–56. Hillsdale, NJ: Lawrence Erlbaum.

Fawson, P., and R. Reutzel. 2000. "But I Only Have a Basal: Implementing Guided Reading in the Early Grades." *Reading Teacher* 54 (1): 84–97.

Folger, T. 2001. Readers' Parallel Text Construction While Talking and Thinking About the Reading Process. Doctoral diss., University of Missouri, Columbia.

Fountas, I., and G. S. Pinnell. 1996. *Guided Reading: Good First Teaching for All Children*. Portsmouth, NH: Heinemann.

Garan, E. 2002. *Resisting Reading Mandates: How to Triumph with the Truth*. Portsmouth, NH: Heinemann.

Gilles, C., and J. Dickinson. 2000. "Rejoining the Literacy Club: Valuing Middle Grade Readers." *Language Arts* 77 (6): 512–22.

Goodlad, John. 1984. *A Place Called School*. New York: McGraw-Hill.

Goodman, D. 1996. "The Reading Detective Club." In *Retrospective Miscue Analysis: Revaluing Readers and Reading*, ed. Y. M. Goodman and A. M. Marek, 177–87. Katonah, NY: Richard C. Owen.

Goodman, K. S. 1968. "Study of Children's Behavior While Reading Orally." Contract No. OE-6-10-136. Washington, DC: Department of Health, Education, and Welfare.

———. 1969. "Linguistics in a Relevant Curriculum." *Education* 89: 303–6.

———. 1973. "Miscues: Windows on the Reading Process." In *Miscue Analysis: Applications to Reading Instruction*, ed. K. S. Goodman, 3–14. Urbana, IL: ERIC Clearinghouse on Reading and Communication Skills and National Council of Teachers of English.

———. 1984. "Unity in Reading." In *Becoming Readers in a Complex Society*, ed. A. C. Purves and O. Niles, 79–114. Chicago: University of Chicago Press.

———. 1994. "Reading, Writing, and Written Texts: A Transactional Socio-Psycholinguistic View." In *Theoretical Models and Process of Reading*, ed. R. B. Ruddell, M. R. Ruddell, and H. Singer, 1093–1130. 4th ed. Newark, DE: National Council of Teachers of English.

———. 1996a. *Ken Goodman: On Reading*. Portsmouth, NH: Heinemann.

————. 1996b. "Principles of Revaluing." In *Retrospective Miscue Analysis: Revaluing Readers and Reading,* ed. Y. M. Goodman and A. M. Marek, 13–20. Katonah, NY: Richard C. Owen.

Goodman, Y. M. 1995. "Miscue Analysis for Classroom Teachers: Some History and Some Procedures." *Primary Voices K–6* 3 (4): 2–9.

————. 1996. "Revaluing Readers While Readers Revalue Themselves: Retrospective Miscue Analysis." *The Reading Teacher* 49 (8): 600–609.

Goodman, Y. M., and A. Flurkey. 1996. "Retrospective Miscue Analysis in the Middle School." In *Retrospective Miscue Analysis: Revaluing Readers and Reading,* ed. Y. M. Goodman and A. M. Marek, 87–105. Katonah, NY: Richard C. Owen.

Goodman, Y. M., and A. M. Marek. 1989. "Retrospective Miscue Analysis: Two Papers." Occasional Paper No. 19. Tucson, AZ: University of Arizona, College of Education, Program in Language and Literacy.

————. 1996. *Retrospective Miscue Analysis: Revaluing Readers and Reading.* Katonah, NY: Richard C. Owen.

Goodman, Y. M., D. J. Watson, and C. L. Burke. 1987. *Reading Miscue Inventory: Alternative Procedures.* New York: Richard C. Owen.

————. 2005. *Reading Miscue Inventory: From Evaluation to Instruction for All Readers.* New York: Richard C. Owen.

Gore, J. 1993. *The Struggle for Pedagogies.* New York: Routledge.

Halliday, M. A. K. 1980. "Three Aspects of Children's Language Development: Learning Language, Learning Through Language, Learning About Language." In *Oral and Written Language Development Research: Impact on the Schools,* ed. Y. Goodman, M. Haussler, and D. Strickland, 7–20. Urbana, IL: IRA and NCTE Joint Publications.

Harp, B. 2000. *The Handbook of Literacy Assessment and Evaluation.* 2d ed. Norwood, MA: Christopher-Gordon.

Henson, J., and C. Gilles. 2003. "Al's Story: Overcoming Beliefs That Inhibit Learning." *Language Arts* 8: 259–68.

Hinchman, K., and P. Michel. 1999. "Reconciling Polarity: Toward a Responsive Model of Evaluating Literacy Performance." *Reading Teacher* 52: 578–87.

Kaplan, A., and M. L. Maehr. 1997. "School Cultures." In *Psychology and Educational Practice,* ed. H. J. Walberg and G. D. Haertal, 342–55. Berkeley, CA: McClutchan.

Keene, E., and S. Zimmermann. 1997. *Mosaic of Thought.* Portsmouth, NH: Heinemann.

Leslie, L., and J. Caldwell. 1988. *Qualitative Reading Inventory.* New York: Harper Collins.

Lindfors, J. 1991. *Children's Language and Learning.* Needham Heights, MA: Allyn and Bacon.

Marek, A. M. 1987. Retrospective Miscue Analysis as an Instructional Strategy with Adult Readers. Doctoral diss., University of Arizona.

Martens, P. 1998. "Using Retrospective Miscue Analysis to Inquire: Learning from Michael." *Reading Teacher* 52 (2): 176–80.

Mehan, H. 1979. *Learning Lessons*. Cambridge, MA: Harvard University Press.

Moore, R. A. 2003. *Classroom Research for Teachers: A Practical Guide*. Norwood, MA: Christopher-Gordon.

Moore, R. A., and C. Aspegren. 2000. Reaching Troubled Readers with RMA. Paper presented at the annual meeting of the International Reading Association, Indianapolis.

———. 2001. "Reflective Conversations Between Two Learners: Retrospective Miscue Analysis." *Journal of Adolescent and Adult Literacy* 44 (6): 492–503.

Moore, R. A., and K. Brantingham. 2003. "Nathan: A Case Study in Retrospective Miscue Analysis." *Reading Teacher* 56 (5): 466–74.

Moustafa, M. 1997. *Beyond Traditional Phonics*. Portsmouth, NH: Heinemann.

Pahls-Weiss, Mary. 2002. A Study of the Use of Retrospective Miscue Analysis with Selected First Grade Readers. Doctoral diss., University of Missouri, Columbia.

Pearson, P. David, and M. C. Gallagher. 1983. "The Instruction of Reading Comprehension." *Contemporary Educational Psychology* 8: 317–44.

Pierce, K., and C. Gilles, eds. 1993. *Cycles of Meaning: Exploring the Potential of Talk in Learning Communities*. Portsmouth, NH: Heinemann.

Pinnell, G. S., and I. Fountas. 2000. *Word Matters*. Portsmouth, NH: Heinemann.

Reutzel, R., and R. Cooter. 2003. *Strategies for Reading Assessment and Instruction*. 2d ed. Upper Saddle River, NJ: Pearson Education.

Rosenblatt, L. [1938] 1976. *Literature as Exploration*. New York: Noble and Noble.

———. 1978. *The Reader, the Text, the Poem: The Transactional Theory of the Literary Work*. Carbondale, IL: Southern Illinois University Press.

Smith, F. 1994. *Understanding Reading: A Psycholinguistic Analysis of Reading and Learning to Read*. 5th ed. Hillsdale, NJ: Erlbaum.

Strickland, K., and J. Strickland. 2000. *Making Assessment Elementary*. Portsmouth, NH: Heinemann.

Tovani, C. 2000. *I Read It, But I Don't Get It*. Portland, ME: Stenhouse.

Vygotsky, L. 1978. *Mind in Society: The Development of Higher Psychological Processes*. Cambridge, MA: Harvard University Press.

Watson, D. J. 1978. "Reader-Selected Miscues: Getting More from Sustained Silent Reading." *English Education* 10: 75–85.

———. 1988. "Knowing Where We're Coming From." In *Whole Language Strategies for Secondary Students*, ed. C. Gilles, M. Bixby, P. Crowley, S. Crenshaw, M. Henrichs, F. Reynolds, and D. Pyle, 3–10. New York: Richard C. Owen.

———. 1996a. "Miscue Analysis for Teachers." In *Making a Difference: Selected Writings of Dorothy Watson*, ed. Sandra Wilde, 34–55. Portsmouth, NH: Heinemann.

———. 1996b. "Miscues We Have Known and Loved." In *Making a Difference: Selected Writings of Dorothy Watson*, ed. Sandra Wilde, 13–20. Portsmouth, NH: Heinemann.

Watson, D. J., C. Burke, and Y. Goodman. 1988. "Pragmatic and Linguistic Systems of Language." In *Whole Language Strategies*, ed. C. Gilles, M. Bixby, T. Crowley, S. Crenshaw, M. Henrichs, F. Reynolds, and D. Pyle. Portsmouth, NH: Heinemann.

Watson, D. J., and S. Hoge. 1996. "Reader Selected Miscues." In *Retrospective Miscue Analysis: Revaluing Readers and Reading*, ed. Y. M. Goodman and A. M. Marek, 157–64. Katonah, NY: Richard C. Owen.

Weaver, C. 1980. *Psycholinguistics and Reading: From Process to Practice*. Cambridge, MA: Winthrop.

———. 1994. *Reading Process and Practice: From Socio-Psycholinguistics to Whole Language*. Portsmouth, NH: Heinemann.

Weaver, C., L. Gillmeister-Krause, and G. Vento-Zogby, 1996. *Creating Support for Effective Literacy Instruction*. Portsmouth, NH: Heinemann.

Wells, G. 1986. *The Meaning Makers: Children Learning Language and Using Language to Learn*. Portsmouth, NH: Heinemann.

Wells, G., and L. Chang-Wells. 1992. *Constructing Knowledge Together: Classrooms as Centers of Inquiry and Literacy*. Portsmouth, NH: Heinemann.

Wilde, S. 1997. *What's a Schwa Sound Anyway?* Portsmouth, NH: Heinemann.

Worsnop, C. 1980. "A Procedure for Using the Technique of the Reading Miscue Inventory as a Remedial Teaching Tool with Adolescents." ERIC Document ED 324644.

———. 1996. "The Beginnings of Retrospective Miscue Analysis." In *Retrospective Miscue Analysis: Revaluing Readers and Reading,* ed. Y. M. Goodman and A. M. Marek, 151–56. Katonah, NY: Richard C. Owen.

Children's Books Cited

Clements, A. 1996. *Frindle*. New York: Simon and Schuster Books for Young Readers.

Earle, A. 1997. *Zipping, Zapping, Zooming Bats*. Boston: Houghton Mifflin.

Gardiner, J. 1983. *Stone Fox*. New York: Harper Collins Children's.

Howard, E. F. 1995. *Aunt Flossie's Hats (and Crab Cakes Later)*. New York: Clarion.

O'Brien, P. 2000. *The Hindenburg*. New York: Henry Holt.

Rowling, J. K. 1998. *Harry Potter and the Sorcerer's Stone*. New York: Scholastic.

Sachar, L. 1998. *Holes*. New York: Farrar, Straus, and Giroux.

White, E. B. 1952. *Charlotte's Web*. New York: Harper Collins.

Index